County of Warren,

County, that two certain Negro

Mat, have absented themse

re lurking about in the Count

These are therefore in the Name of

s forthwith to surrender them

And We do hereby also requ

n, to make diligent Search

Slaves, and them having foun

may be conveyed to their said

The Kinsey Collection

Thanks for being a part of
the Journey...

Shirley

Bernard

Khalil

CH

Bernard and Shirley Kinsey, 2002
Artis Lane
Oil on canvas
41 ¾ x 31 ¾ in.

Khalil Kinsey, 1991
Artis Lane
Oil on canvas
40 x 30 in.

Aaron

Enjoy learning
about our History
& culture

Best Wishes

Bernard

The Kinsey Collection

Shared Treasures of Bernard and Shirley Kinsey

Where Art and History Intersect

Bernard W. Kinsey and Shirley Pooler Kinsey

with a foreword by
Douglas A. Blackmon

and an essay by
Khalil B. Kinsey

The Bernard and Shirley Kinsey Foundation for Arts and Education

Casebound edition: ISBN 978-0-9826225-2-0
Collector's edition in slipcase: ISBN 978-0-9826225-3-7
Third Printing (revised and expanded)

Published by: The Bernard and Shirley Kinsey Foundation for Arts and Education
              The Kinsey Collection.
              PO Box 1730
              Pacific Palisades, CA 90272-1730
              book@thekinseycollection.com

Made possible by the generous support of
Edison International-Southern California Edison
Toyota Motor Sales, USA, Inc.
Farmers Insurance Group
United Parcel Service of America, Inc.
Northrop Grumman Foundation
Southwest Airlines

Authors: Bernard W. and Shirley Pooler Kinsey
Contributing writers: Douglas Blackmon, Khalil B. Kinsey
Research, catalogue entries: Bernard W. Kinsey, Khalil B. Kinsey
Additional research, curatorial services, and preliminary copy: Jill Moniz, PhD
Art Consultant: Terry Harris

Producer: Charles Allen
Production design: Howard Morris
Prepress and Print Management: Charles Allen Imaging Experts, Pasadena, CA
Printed and bound in South Korea

Jacket and end sheet illustrations:
Front inside jacket: *Bernard and Shirley Kinsey, 2002,* Artis Lane, oil on canvas
Well-to-do black couple, ca. 1860, maker unknown, hand-colored tintype

Back inside jacket: Individual three-dimensional portraits of Bernard, Shirley, and Khalil Kinsey, 2008, Mikel Alatza,
oil on board

Endsheets: Section of Arrest Proclamation for Jem and Mat, escaped slaves, issued by Warren County, NC, 1798

For further information or to purchase copies: www.thekinseycollection.com

This book is dedicated to those whose paths have brought us here, and whose lives have shaped ours; we are forever indebted to them.

With special thanks from Shirley

To Erma Lee Lofton Pooler, the mother I never got to know but whose presence I feel with every breath.

To Eddie James Pooler, my dad. Thank you for being you.

And to Susie Plummer Pooler, my grandmother, "Mama," who gave me wings and then pushed me to fly.

I love you and can never thank you enough.

With special thanks from Bernard

To Ulysses B. Kinsey, my dad, who taught me respect, honor, and the value of education.

To Christine Stiles Kinsey, my mom, who taught me the importance of financial responsibility and family.

Together, you gave me the foundation to build a skyscraper and showed me what a true love and partnership can do. Thank you.

Contents

Foreword

Not long after my book, *Slavery by Another Name: The Re-Enslavement of Black Americans from the Civil War to World War II*, was published in 2008, I received an unexpected call from Bernard Kinsey. He insisted that he was a direct relative of a woman whose poignant letter of 1903 to President Theodore Roosevelt appeared prominently in the book.

The letter, written by a then-young woman named Carrie Kinsey, described how her 14-year-old brother had been kidnapped and sold into slavery. It was the historical artifact that had haunted me more than any other in the eight-year process of writing my book, and I'd never been able to learn the fates of Carrie or James. In just a few desperate lines, written in the struggling hand of a barely literate, impoverished African American woman, was a story that distilled both the individual horror and the fantastic width and breadth of the American campaign to crush Southern blacks at the beginning of the 20th century. I later told Bernard that in the story of Carrie's stolen brother James—his seizure and sale to a massive plantation owned by one of Georgia's most powerful families, the abject refusal of authorities to assist her, the brutalization of thousands of other blacks on the plantation where he worked in chains, the heroism of Carrie Kinsey in seeking the aid of President Roosevelt, and finally in the futility of her never investigated letter—was the entire epic tragedy of black life in the rural South at that time. All the wrongs, all the valiance of African Americans who persevered against immeasurable odds, all the failings of America to the slaves emancipated by the Civil War and to generations of their descendants.

Bernard pleaded for a copy of the full text of the letter. He wanted to include it in exhibitions of the Kinsey Collection. But weeks passed without my fulfilling his request. I told myself that I was delaying because the letter was filed away with thousands of other things, then that I was swamped by the surprising response to my book—as I was eventually awarded a Pulitzer Prize. Weeks passed. Bernard called and e-mailed again. Finally I realized that I was avoiding the letter for another reason: my own personal sense of shame. Not shame for anything I had done personally. But shame for America—for white Americans first but also for all of America. Shame that an idealistic nation could expend so much of its own blood to give freedom and citizenship and opportunity to four million enslaved African Americans and then allow that achievement to be debased in barely the span of a generation.

Finally one Saturday morning, I dug through the boxes, found the letter, and sent it to him. A few months later, I escorted him and his extraordinary wife Shirley to the National Archives. In an intensely emotional moment we each held in our hands the actual piece of paper that 106 years earlier had been in the hands of Carrie Kinsey, the paper on which she inked perhaps the only record of the life and loss of her brother James.

Such humble artifacts are crucial to our understanding of the past, and of ourselves. Major documents and official histories almost always survive to tell the story of society's rulers. But only through the miraculously preserved wisps of history like Carrie Kinsey's letter can we defy the inexorable erasure of the full story of all our forebears. Bernard and Shirley Kinsey understand that. By the time we held the Carrie Kinsey letter in our hands together, I had come to know them as friends—and had heard the remarkable story of their lives and their fantastic achievements, professionally, personally, and as chroniclers of the African American experience.

I learned from them that Carrie Kinsey's family survived its ordeal to become key leaders among African Americans. The letter—like the entire Kinsey Collection—came also to represent for me something altogether different. It is a totem of a story of the greatest kind of American triumph, of a family besieged but never destroyed by the worst forces of our society. Of a family that survived and then thrived—and now seeks to share a legacy of comprehension and appreciation of the African American experience.

There are few forces in America that more powerfully demonstrate how much can be achieved in our country—and has been achieved by African Americans—than Bernard and Shirley Kinsey and their extraordinary collection.

— Douglas A. Blackmon

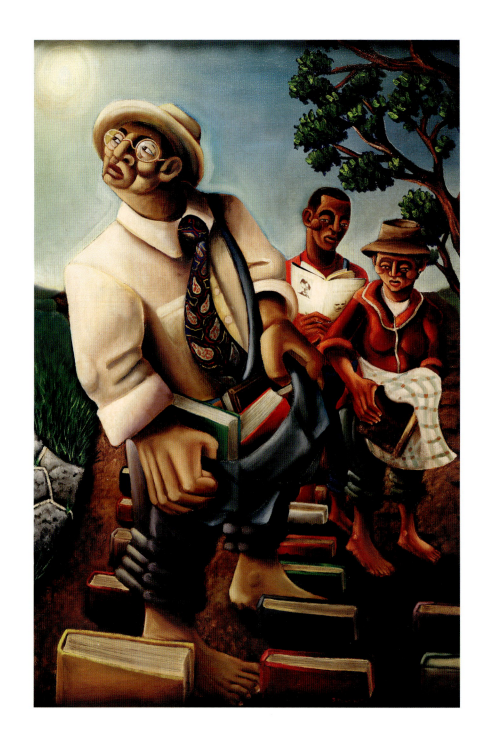

The Cultivators, 2000
Samuel L. Dunson, Jr.
Oil on canvas
38 ½ x 26 ½ in.

Introduction

We strive to live our life guided by two principles: *To whom much is given much is required,* and *a life of no regrets.* We believe in the notion of giving back, so we decided to share our 35-year life of collecting the African American experience and culture through historical documents, manuscripts, photographs, paintings, and sculpture.

As our life together has evolved, so too has our collecting. Shirley has been clear from the start that we should tell a positive story of African American accomplishments and triumphs rather than concentrating on the despicable history of oppression that haunts black people and this country. We have put our primary focus on creating educational opportunities by displaying the complexity and beauty of African American life, which our collection encompasses.

We believe strongly that vibrant cultural communities need venues for displaying and sharing art as well as patrons to support them. Museums provide extraordinary opportunities to explore the intersections of art and history, and we are grateful to the institutions that have proudly exhibited our collection. This has enabled tens of thousands of people to interact with artifacts and art that have helped shape a nation.

Our exhibit's journey began in Los Angeles at the California African American Museum (CAAM) as "In the Hands of African American Collectors: The Personal Treasures of Bernard and Shirley Kinsey." After a five-month run and an overwhelmingly positive response, the exhibit grew wings. We have had the opportunity to listen to visitors who saw the exhibition in Cincinnati at the National Underground Railroad Freedom Center, in Chicago at the DuSable Museum of African American History, in West Palm Beach, Florida, at the Norton Museum of Art, in Tallahassee at the Mary Brogan Museum of Art and Science, and at the Smithsonian National Museum of American History in Washington, D.C., where over two million people viewed the collection.

In response to what we have heard, in concert with our own evolving purpose, we decided to shift the emphasis of the narrative to the African American experience as told through our perspective, shaped by 43 years of marriage. This resulted in expanding and redesigning the exhibit and in the production of this book, *The Kinsey Collection: Shared Treasures of Bernard and Shirley Kinsey, Where Art and History Intersect.* The book includes pieces that are not shown in the exhibit, but are very important to us and to the story.

Shirley and I have been blessed beyond measure and always felt it our obligation to share these blessings to help others. This moral compass has driven our collecting and our desire to share this work. We know that in order for history to have social value it needs to be personal and intimate, revealing the passions and problems of people in the past so that it connects with the present, enabling history to come alive.

The story we highlight in our collection shows what we have learned about ourselves and our history, particularly that black people have been a part of everything that has happened in the Americas from the beginning. The impact and influence of African Americans on American history is often taken for granted and overlooked, though in fact nearly everything from the 17th through the 19th centuries was built by African Americans. The ultimate example of this is our nation's capital, Washington, D.C., where African Americans built the White House and the Capitol and contributed to the layout of the entire city.

We have worked hard to add our voice to the many voices dedicated to shining a light on the wonderful story of the African American experience. Our intention is that this book inspire people to develop a deeper relationship to the pieces in our collection, and to the history that it brings to life. Having that connection with the past creates this sense of strength, identity, and lineage that is so powerful in us. Over the past 35 years we have become caretakers of this body of work, and we share with you our thoughts, aspirations, and perceptions at this intersection of art and history. This book is part of an ever evolving road of discovery for us and we invite you to join us on the journey.

— Bernard W. & Shirley Pooler Kinsey

Understanding the Past Part I: A Personal Perspective

I grew up in the South in the 1950s and '60s, in a solid middle-class family. With my dad, who was a principal, and my stay-at-home mom and five siblings, I lived in West Palm Beach, Florida, in a totally segregated world.

I was born and raised in public housing, "the projects." It was simply where everyone lived: the teachers, the postman, the gardeners. Everyone enjoyed their housing, regardless of their class. Everything and anybody that was necessary and important to me was located in our community between 1st and 25th Streets and the two railroad tracks.

My family treasured music, books, achievement, and thrift, all of which grounded my brothers and sisters and me. My dad, U.B. Kinsey, was a civil rights legend in Palm Beach County, for he refused to accept the strictures of segregation, Jim Crow, or mediocrity. For 39 years, he was the principal at Palmview Elementary School, which now bears his name, and he was active in every fight for better conditions for blacks in West Palm Beach.

In 1941, Dad and a group of black educators sued the Palm Beach County school board in a case seeking equal pay for black teachers and equal education for black students. The traditional school calendar lasted from September to June, but typically in the South, black students followed a January to June calendar and were required to do farm labor for the rest of the year. Thurgood Marshall, the attorney who argued on their behalf and won, later used the precedent to attack *Plessy v. Ferguson*, which led to the *Brown v. Board of Education* ruling of 1954.

My dad fought for the black community to have sewers, streetlights, sidewalks, landscaping, and to his credit, the black community is still beautiful today, with well kept lawns and homes. Growing up in a home with a strong, courageous, and loving father made a big impression on me, particularly watching Dad live by his motto, "Stand for Right." He consistently did so, in our segregated community and beyond.

My mom remains the consummate homemaker. Juggling our family finances on a black teacher's salary during the 1940s and '50s taught me the value of a dollar, how to save, and how to take care of what you own. Mom would go to three grocery stores with a coupon wallet to ensure that we got the best value for our purchases. These fiscal lessons anchor how Shirley and I live our lives.

Education was very important in our family. Mom and Dad met in college, Florida A&M University in Tallahassee, and later married and moved to West Palm Beach. I attended Palmview Elementary, Roosevelt High School, then my parents' alma mater.

Every year, one of the most important football games in America was the Orange Blossom Classic, played in Miami between Florida A&M University and the top black college team for the Negro national championship. The game typically drew 40,000 fans, including Mom and Dad, who would take all of us. It was there that I saw the Florida A&M University "Marching 100" and decided on the spot that I would go to FAMU and play in the band.

After a very successful high school career, where I was class president, I entered FAMU in 1961. By 1964, Mom and Dad had four kids in college at the same time. It was years later that I learned how much they sacrificed to send us to college, and recognized the indelible stamp of promise that education is for the American dream, even more so for black Americans.

FAMU had a profound impact on my life in many ways. I met Shirley, the best part of my day, and many of our closest friends, including Nick Walker, Mike Williams, and Thomas Mitchell. My relationships with the directors of the Marching 100, Dr. William P. Foster and Dr. Julian White, and other faculty and administrators enabled me to develop the leadership and interpersonal skills I needed to compete effectively in the white world I soon entered.

One professor who had an influence on me that I realized only much later was Dr. James Eaton, a professor of history. He founded the Black Archives on campus and was the keeper of all things FAMU, as well as documenting the struggle and achievements of people of color in Florida and elsewhere in the South. In class he would say, "There would be no history in this country if it weren't for black folks. African American history is American history."

Going to college in the '60s helped shape my attitudes and values about being black. For many years I struggled with the notion of American segregation and racism, and always wanted to know how black people in this country got into this predicament. Dr. Eaton's saying stuck with me for many years, and through travel, study, and reading I came to know what he meant. We have been here from the beginning and we have a story to tell that all Americans must know. Each of us must engage with the history and continue the narrative.

My commitment to civil rights has taken many forms over the past four decades, from my days in college, protesting segregated conditions, to Xerox, where I helped shape the company and hired thousands of African Americans, Latinos, and women. My work as co-chair of Rebuild LA attracted nearly $400 million in new capital to rebuild the city after the 1992 uprising, and Shirley and I have worked together to raise over $20 million for community organizations and for educational scholarships to historically black colleges. Now we are sharing the wonderful story of our ancestors' struggles, triumphs, and accomplishments through *The Kinsey Collection: Shared Treasures of Bernard and Shirley Kinsey, Where Art and History Intersect*. My understanding of my parents' efforts and Dr. Eaton's lessons is embodied here in this book, through my personal history, my collecting, and my own words.

— Bernard W. Kinsey

Understanding the Past Part II: Collecting History

Shirley and I have been married for 44 years. Our journey together is filled with experiences we cherish: the birth of our son, Khalil, travel, learning, and sharing our personal history with friends and our community. We enjoy discovering new places and ideas, and we have focused our education on our past. Shirley documents our personal history through visual and written reminders. I concentrate on exploring books and historical facts that affirm the perseverance of people of color and their contributions to the world. For example, Leo Africanus' *Description of Africa* (1550)—represented in our collection in a Latin edition of 1632—supports the view that Africa was not a "dark" continent but a very sophisticated civilization that practiced astronomy, medicine, and science.

We owe a great deal to historians and scholars whose research teaches us about what we collect. Bibliophile Charles Blockson compiled *A Commented Bibliography of 101 Influential Books by and about People of African Descent (1556–1982)*, a work that became my bible in discovering and collecting stories of our people. Henry Proctor Slaughter, Dr. Dorothy Porter Wesley, Arthur Schomburg, Carter G. Woodson, Alain Locke, and John Wesley Cromwell, Sr., are all owed a deep debt of gratitude for preserving our heritage through books, pamphlets, and documents. These authors make the discovery of the African American past possible.

Kenneth M. Stampp's *The Peculiar Institution: Slavery in the Ante-Bellum South* has influenced the modern understanding of slavery and my own thinking on the subject. John Hope Franklin's groundbreaking book *From Slavery to Freedom* and Herbert Aptheker's writings documenting the slave revolts beginning in the 17th century have exploded the myth that black people accepted their fate. Through these works, we encountered people who resisted their bondage, who lived by cunning, courage, even genius, longing to be free. Until I read Franklin's book, like most people, I viewed our history backwards, seeing slavery as an isolated event essentially occurring in the South, when in truth slavery dominated every aspect of American life: politics, economy, religion, social mores, and laws in both North and South.

Against this backdrop, Shirley and I have set about telling a story of the African American experience. We want to give our ancestors voices, names, and personalities so that we and others can better understand their triumphs and accomplishments, despite the challenges and obstacles they faced, and the extraordinary sacrifices they made building this country.

The evidence of African American survival and prosperity is available through many different media, including documentary film and video; in university, state, and national archives; and in scholarly journals and books. These resources provide context for many of the pieces that we have collected and those we would like to acquire and steward. We know from our

own experiences and study that learning about African American accomplishments and struggles contributes to better interracial understanding and tolerance.

Researching in various media, I learned that in 1640, farmer Hugh Gwyn's servants escaped to Maryland. A Dutchman, a Scot, and a black man, John Punch, were all punished for the same crime. The Dutchman and the Scot had their indentures extended by one year while John Punch was sentenced to slavery for life. It was John Punch's color that doomed him to a life of enslavement. This record of enslavement dramatically changed the social, political, and economic landscape of America. Its effects can still be felt today.

Our first historical document was a gift that encouraged me on this mission of collecting and sharing these experiences with others. It was an 1832 bill of sale for William Johnson, who was sold for $550, the equivalent of $14,000 today. As I held this document in my hand, it was as if I was holding him and all that had gone before him in this terrible existence called slavery. It profoundly changed my life and my understanding of what I could discover about myself, my ancestors, and African American history.

What really interests me is getting underneath the traditional definitions of historical events and documents, in order to provide an alternative point of view. By displaying artifacts that show African American perspectives, I hope to dispel the myths that still prevail about black contributions—about family, hard work, and

genius; about Jim Crow and the courage of our people. It is important to be able to connect scholarship to tangible artifacts that document this history, so that it can be seen and known in another way. One little-known and fascinating story concerns Antonio and Isabela Tucker, who came to this continent in 1619 as indentured servants rather than slaves. They earned their freedom, married, and had a son, William, born in 1625, who was the first child of African parents baptized in Jamestown. Black family life has its roots in an era that long preceded the institution of slavery and its concomitant denegration of the black family.

Another important contribution to American life that needs more attention is the work of Phillis Wheatley. Many people don't know that she was a brilliant writer who at that time was as popular as Oprah Winfrey is today. She arrived a tattered young girl on a slave ship and became a literary force who read for the Founding Fathers, including Benjamin Franklin.

I am interested in the early work of black businessmen, particularly Philadelphian James Forten, who amassed an estate of over $100 thousand. One of the earliest black abolitionists, as well as one of the earliest successful black entrepreneurs, he managed one of the first known integrated work forces in America, with an almost even division between black and white workers in a city that had experienced frequent racial violence. Although virtually unknown today, Forten made a tremendous contribution to the fabric of this country. We do not possess any artifacts that tell his story, but it is one that very much needs to be told. I include him in the exhibition catalogue for this reason.

Then there are the Buffalo Soldiers, the most decorated unit in American military history. They received eighteen Congressional Medals of Honor, including five for the taking of San Juan Hill. Among them is Henry Flipper, the first black man to graduate from West Point, who in 1877 left the institution without having been spoken to in four years. One of the first superintendents of Yosemite National Park was Buffalo Soldier Colonel Charles Young. These are our heroes.

Share the wealth of African American experience in these pages and in our exhibition as it travels the nation. Use public libraries and universities to connect with history in a personal way and discover your own heroes to add to the story.

— Bernard W. Kinsey

***Door of No Return**, 2007*
Courtesy of documentary photographer
Kwesi Hutchful

Lineage

Truth is powerful and it prevails.
— Sojourner Truth

The Bernard and Shirley Kinsey Collection contains a wide range of art and artifacts that bear witness to the multi-layered intersections of the past and present. From a curatorial perspective, the correlations of seemingly disparate objects and their historical moments yield a holistic understanding of the Kinseys' mission. In aggregate these intersections, though sometimes confrontational, become a celebration of the diversity of African and African American experience in the world.

Yet the artifacts represented in this volume tell a story that is far from comforting. The context of each piece is complex, shedding light on the difficulties of being black but also illuminating the brilliance of exceptional people whose contributions add enduring force to the often undervalued collective history of a people. The Kinseys themselves are included in this oeuvre because their vision supports this agenda: amassing objects that can be juxtaposed, sometimes in surprising ways, in order to illuminate the past.

The Kinseys value roots. Florida is the beginning of their personal stories, where they were raised, met, and began their journey together. The beginning of their cultural cosmology, however, lies in Africa, in the extraordinary stories of men and women who overcame the harsh realities of discrimination and slavery to prosper, or simply to survive. The Kinseys are determined to preserve the earliest documentations of the collision between Africans and those who sought to possess them.

During much of modern American history, people were taught that African slaves were from a "dark" continent and lacked both technical expertise and culture. But these myths, created to ensure subservience and racial stratification, could not be further from the truth. The same myths served to misrepresent the true impact of the vast numbers of Africans brought from the continent to Europe and the New World.

Bernard and Shirley Kinsey collect ephemera, including books, ledgers, accounts, and artifacts used in the transatlantic slave trade. These provide tangible evidence of both the single-mindedness of the European imperialist agenda and the intellectual acuity of the unfortunate Africans who were victims of that brutal agenda. The African and European artifacts shown here exemplify an intersection of worlds at the historical moments that brought black people to the shores of Europe and the New World, where they were considered assets and commodities to be counted, traded, and sold.

African men and women, however, understood and accommodated the complex and often hostile world around them, in ways that allowed them to produce and prosper. Their work provides telling evidence of their dedication to the pursuit of freedom and knowledge, and examples of an extraordinary aesthetics that captivated those who sought to capture and control them.

The Kinseys' personal journey began over a century after the official cessation of the transatlantic slave trade, but the history of the legacy of courage in the face of disenfranchisement begins here.

Gorée Island Rock, n.d.
Gift of Ed Dwight to Bernard and Shirley Kinsey
3 x 10 x 6 ½ in.

This rock was a gift to the Kinseys from an artist who traveled to Gorée, a small island located off the coast of Senegal in western Africa. Although the island was only a minor slave port, it has become famous for La Maison des Esclaves (The Slave House), constructed in 1786 by French African Creoles. The house continues to stand as a testament to the history of the slave trade in the region. Now a museum displaying slavery artifacts, it contains the "Door of No Return," an example of the portal through which millions of slaves left African shores bound for a life of servitude in the New World. Bernard traces the family's ancestors to Senegal and this rock represents the passage of those ancestors to the Americas.

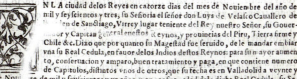

PARA QVE SE APRE-
MIEN, LOS ESPAÑOLES
BALDIOS, MESTIZOS, MVLATOS,
Negros, y çambahigos se alquilen y siruan.
(.?.)

DE OFFICIO.

AVTO.

N LA ciudad delos Reyes en catorze dias del mes de Nouiembre del año de mil y seyscientos y tres, su Señoria el señor don Luys de Velasco Cauallero de en de Sanctiago, Virrey lugar teniente del Rey nuestro Señor, su Gouer- nador y Capitan general enestos Reynos, y prouincias del Piru, Tierra firme y Chile &c. Dixo que por quanto su Magestad fue seruido, de le mandar embiar vna su Real Cedula, en fauor delos Indios destos Reynos: para su mayor aumen to, conseruacion y amparo, buen tratamiento y paga, en que contiene numero de Capitulos, distintos vnos de otros, que su fecha es en Valladolid a veynte y quatro de Noui re, de mil y seyscientos y vn años, y en conformidad dela dicha Real Cedula, su Se ñoria ha mandad despachar algunas Prouisiones, que por agora a parecido ser necessarias, insertos los capitulos dela a Real C ula a ella: tocantes, para que se guarden y cumplan, como su Magestad lo manda, y par poo iar a todo el Reyno, y que se entreguen alos Corregidores: para que las hagan pregonar, publicar, cumplir y executar, (como enellas se contienen, y con el cuydado y diligen- cia, que el caso requiere, y su Magestad lo manda) es necessario, que se publiquen, enesta dicha Ciudad, enla plaça della, y que Antonio Ricardo impressor las imprima, por escusar la dilacion, que podra auer de exercirse tanto numero como se requiere embiar. Para lo qual mandaua, y mando a don Iosephe de Ribera, Corregidor delos Naturales desta ciudad, que con assistencia del Protector, y Procura- dor general de los desté Reyno, y con trompetas y chirimias, enla plaça desta dicha Ciudad, ha- ga publicar y pregonar las dichas Prouisiones, y el Domingo, diez y seys deste presente mes, ansi mes mo enel pueblo del Cercado, haziendo, que esten juntos los mas indios que ser pudiere, y que se les de a entender, y declaren en su Lengua. Y daua y dio licencia al dicho Antonio Ricardo: para que impri- ma las dichas Prouisiones, las quales se guarden, cumplan y executen, como si fueran firmadas de ma no de su Señoria, y refrendadas del Secretario de la Gouernacion deste Reyno, sin que en ello se pon ga escusa alguna, poniendo por cabeça y principio delas dichas Prouisiones este Auto. Don Luys de Velasco. Don Alonso Fernandez de Cordoua.

ON Luis de Velasco, Cauallero dela orden de Sanctia go, Virrey lugar Theniete del Rey nuestro señor, su Go uernador, y Capitan general en estos Reynos, y Prouin- cias del Piru, Tierrafirme, y Chile. &c. Por quanto su Magestad con el gran celo y cuydado, que tiene del bie publico, conseruacion, y augmento de sus Reynos y esta dos, y de que sus vasallos sean mantenidos en paz y justi cia, y abunden de todo aquello que es necessario, y conuiniente ala sustenta cion dela vida humana, considerando de quanta importancia sea para esto, que enlo que fuere pussible enlos dichos sus Reynos no aya gente ociosa y

A valdia,

Para Que Se Apremien, Los Espanoles,
Baldios, Mestizos, Mulatos, Negros,
y cambahijos se alquilen y siruan., 1604
Printed paper
8 ½ x 12 ¼ in.

Official "Cedula," or decree, ordering all Spaniards, Negroes, Mulattoes, Quadroons, and Octoroons who are not employed to re- port for work. Signed by Don Luis de Velasco, by order of the Viceroy, Don Alonso Fernandez de Cordova.

An example of the power of the Inquisition, this order is one of twelve ordinances issued on the same day by Luis de Velasco, and the only one to mention people of color. The ordi- nance stated that those who were enjoying the fruits of the labor of others, while doing nothing themselves to contribute to the gen- eral good in Lima, were ordered to work, and given only a few days to comply. The order was to be enforced "with all the rigor of physical as well as monetary punishments."

This document establishes the fact that Africans have been a part of the development of the Americas from the earliest conquest by the Spanish, Portuguese, French, English, and Dutch. Blacks were with Pizarro in Peru, Cortes in Mexico, Menendez in Florida, and they ac- companied DeSoto. The document also re- veals that Africans were classified during the colonial occupation by the amount of white blood they carried in their veins:

Negro: both parents of African descent
Mulatto: a white parent and a black parent
Quadroon: a mulatto parent and a white parent
Octoroon: a quadroon parent and a white parent

Ioannis Leonis Africani Africae, 1632
De totius Africae descriptione libri IX
Book
4 ¾ x 3 x 2 in.

Al Hassan ibn Mohammed al Wazzan al Fassi was born in 1485 in Granada, Spain. He returned with his parents to their native Morocco and studied at the University of Al-Karaouine, founded in Fez in 859 A.D. In 1518, the ship that carried him home to Morocco after his travels in the Middle East was seized by Spanish Corsairs and taken to Rome, where he was received and baptized by Pope Leo X and renamed Leo Africanus. He was freed when his captors realized he was from a prominent diplomatic family and could be a useful ally. Africanus traveled extensively throughout Italy for several years, then returned to Rome under the protection of Pope Clement VII. In 1526, he completed _Ioannis Leonis Africani Africae,_ detailing African geography, with much of the information gathered from his studies at university and his interaction with African travelers in Egypt. The book is considered to be the first descriptive work on Africa authored by a person of African descent. Very popular long after its original publication, it was translated in the early 17th century from Arabic into several languages, including Latin and French. This edition, of 1632, is in Latin.

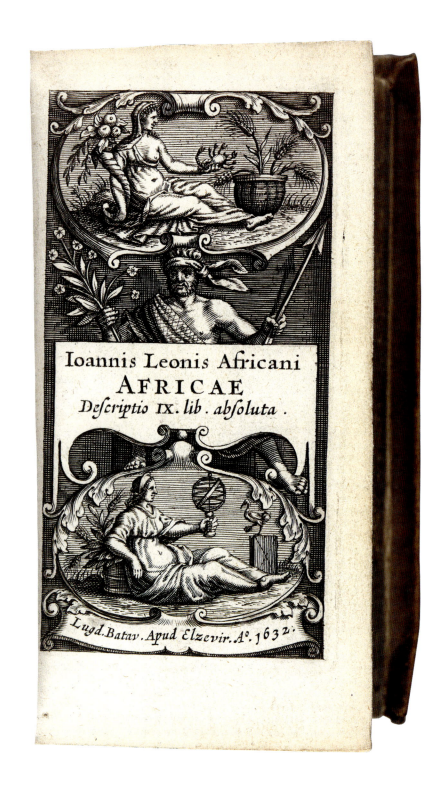

Ioannis Leonis Africani
AFRICAE
Deſcriptio IX. lib. abſoluta.

Lugd. Batav. Apud Elzevir. Aº. 1632.

TRACTATUS

PACIS & AMICITIÆ

INTER

Sereniſſimam ac Potentiſſimam Principem ANNAM, Dei Gratiâ, Magnæ Britanniæ, Eranciæ, & Hiberniæ, Reginam, Fidei Defenſorem, &c. & Sereniſſimum ac Potentiſſimum Principem PHILIPPUM V. Dei Gratiâ, Hiſpaniarum Regem Catholicum, Concluſus Trajecti ad Rhenum die $\frac{2}{13}$ Menſis Julii, Anno 1713.

TREATY

OF

PEACE and FRIENDSHIP

BETWEEN

The moſt Serene and moſt Potent Princeſs A N N E, by the Grace of God, Queen of Great Britain, France, and Ireland, Defender of the Faith, &c. and the moſt Serene and moſt Potent Prince PHILIP the Vth, the Catholick King of Spain, Concluded at Utrecht the $\frac{2}{13}$ Day of July, 1713.

By Her Majeſties Special Command.

SEMPER EADEM

LONDON,

Printed by John Baskett, Printer to the Queens moſt Excellent Majeſty, And by the Aſſigns of Thomas Newcomb, and Henry Hills, deceas'd. 1714.

Treaty of Utrecht, 1714
John Baskett, printer
Excerpt from book
8 ¾ x 7 in.

The Treaties of Utrecht ended the War of Spanish Succession (1701–13) and divided the spoils among Europe's monarchies, following the détente between the English and the French. This treaty grants the United Kingdom a 30-year *asiento* to supply slaves to the Spanish colonies. France would ultimately gain the coveted contract; however, her government, born of a bloody revolution, would in 1794 become the first to declare an official end to slavery and the slave trade.

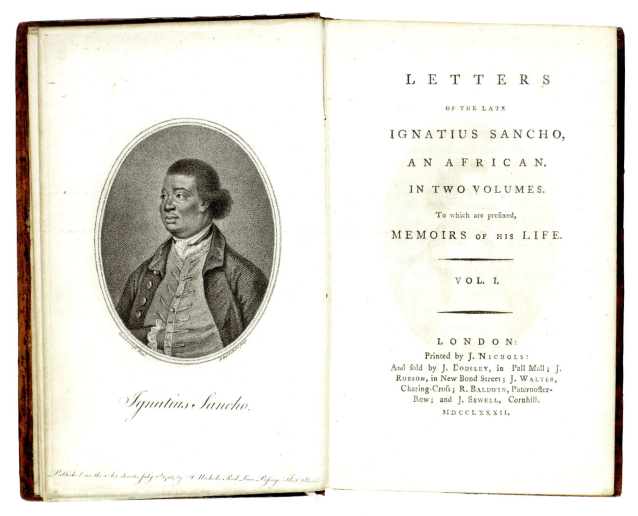

Letters of the Late Ignatius Sancho, an African, in Two Volumes, 1782
Ignatius Sancho
Book
8 x 5 ½ x 2 in.

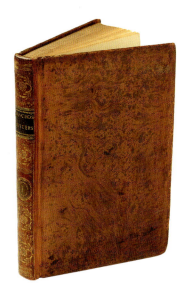

Ignatius Sancho (1729–1780) was born a slave on a ship crossing the Atlantic from Africa to the West Indies. He was taken to Greenwich, England, where he became a butler to the Montagu family, eventually retiring to run a grocery in Westminster. He acted in several plays on the London stage, and is thought to have performed in *Othello*, making him the first black actor to play the Moorish king.

Sancho also composed music and wrote poems and essays, posthumously published in this volume in 1782. The engraved frontispiece is after the portrait of Sancho painted by Thomas Gainsborough. Sancho, known as "The Extraordinary Negro," became a symbol of the humanity of Africans to 18th-century British abolitionists. He was also the first African to vote in a British election.

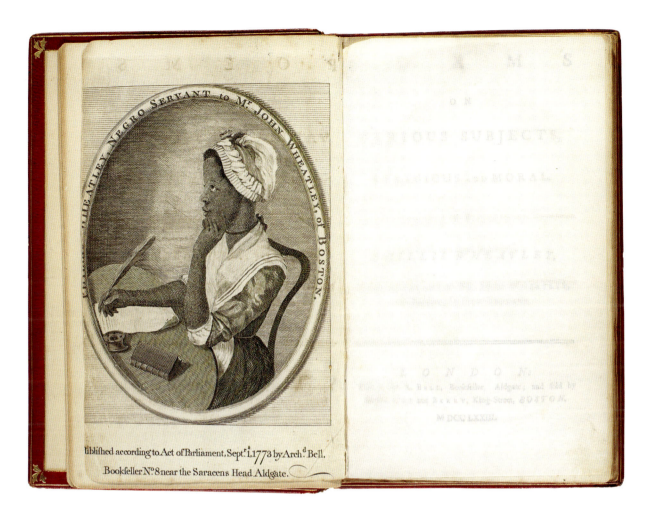

**Poems on Various Subjects
Religious and Moral,** 1773
Phillis Wheatley
Book
7 ¾ x 5 ¼ x 1 ½ in.

Born in Gambia around 1753, Phillis Wheatley was sold into slavery and transported to the New World on the slave ship *Phillis*, after which she was named. In Boston, she was purchased by John Wheatley, a merchant. Wheatley and his wife Susanna educated Phillis and she excelled under their tutelage. She mastered Latin and Greek as well as history and geography, and began writing poetry when she was 13 years old. In 1768, she wrote "To the King's Most Excellent Majesty," dedicated to King George III on the occasion of the repeal of the Stamp Act. Her poems were well received in Boston and London, and she was encouraged by the Countess of Huntingdon to publish a compilation of her work. Many doubted Wheatley's abilities, however, and she had to endure inspection by Boston notables, including John Hancock. In 1773, she finally received her due as a poet, earning recognition from George Washington and Benjamin Franklin.

Wheatley, the "first published African American woman poet, is regarded as a founding figure of black literature. Her portrait printed in the book is the only surviving work by the African American slave artist Scipio Moorhead.

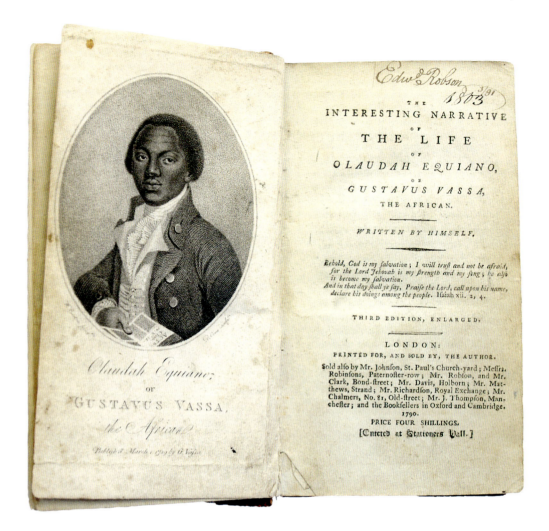

The Interesting Narrative of the Life of Olaudah Equiano, or Gustavus Vassa, The African, 1789
Olaudah Equiano
Book
7 ¼ x 4 ¼ x 1 ¼ in.

A contemporary of Sancho, Olaudah Equiano was captured by African slavers near his home on the Niger River and sold into the transatlantic slave trade. He was purchased by an officer in the British Royal Navy, who taught him seamanship and navigation. Later, Equiano was sold to a Quaker who helped him become more literate and allowed him to buy his freedom. Equiano moved to England to work with William Wilberforce in the abolitionist movement. To promote the cause he wrote of his life as a slave in *The Interesting Narrative of the Life of Olaudah Equiano, or Gustavus Vassa, the African*. This work is one of the few first-person narratives documenting the life of those destined for slavery on the transatlantic slave routes. The book was so popular that six editions quickly followed the initial publication. This book was purchased from Ann Willis, the widow of John Willis, a professor at Princeton, whom Bernard Kinsey never had the chance to meet in person.

Mexican Slave Trade Bill of Sale, 1790
Jose Maria Montano
Ink on paper (4 pages)
12 x 8½ in.

A scarce, early contract of sale in New Spain's slave trade, in which a "mulatto" slave named Jose Maria Montano is sold for sixty pesos.

Since 1492 the history of the Americas has been forged by three cultures: Indigenous, European, and African. It was Africans who established the third root of the Americas, according to Gonzalo Aquirre Beltrán of the University of Veracruz, author of *The Black Population in Mexico* (1964). The first pioneer from Europe to explore what would become the entire southern tier of the United States was an African named Esteban Dorantes (1500–1539). Blacks in the Americas were much more than slaves—they were explorers and co-founders of settlements as far north as Los Angeles, where twenty-six of the forty-four founders were of African descent. The second president of Mexico, Vicente Guerrero, was of African ancestry. He officially abolished slavery in 1822.

Along the Atlantic Coast of the Americas today, 25 percent of the Spanish and Portuguese speaking Latino population is of African descent—a reminder for both communities of their similarities, and for all of us, that racial categorizing does not represent the true facts of human history.

***The History of the Rise, Progress, and Accomplishment of the Abolition of the African Slave-Trade by the British Parliament**, 1808*
Thomas Clarkson, M.A.
Book (2 volumes)
with 2 (one in each volume)
bound and folded nine panel diagrams
8¾ x 5½ in.

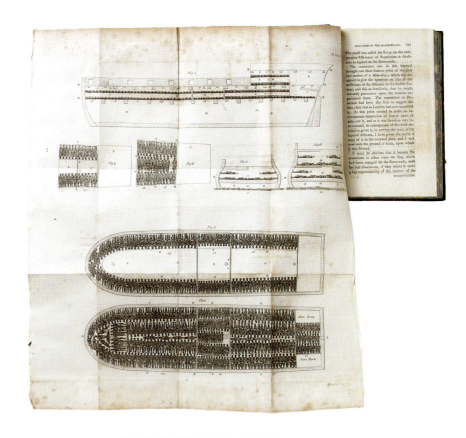

Thomas Clarkson (1760–1846) born in Wisbech, England, became a leading campaigner against the slave trade in the British Empire. Allied with William Wilberforce, Granville Sharp and Josiah Westwood, he was a tireless abolitionist. He helped form the Committee for the Abolition of the Slave Trade in 1787. In 1789 Clarkson was able to promote the Committee's cause by encouraging the sale of the recently published autobiography by the African Olaudah Equiano. Equiano's first-hand account of the slave trade, slavery abroad, and the horrors of the "Middle Passage" demonstrated both literary skill and an unanswerable case against slavery that helped capture the public consciousness.

In three further decades, the slave trade was eliminated in the British Empire and slavery was completely abolished there in 1833. Not until 1865 was slavery ended in America, after what is still the bloodiest war in our history.

Clarkson's book revealed the inhumane treatment Africans suffered in the Transatlantic trade. The diagram shows in dramatic detail the virtual torture that prevailed aboard slave trade ships. Clarkson traveled 35,000 miles on horseback, as he interviewed over 20,000 sailors, seeking the evidence that was to doom slavery and lecturing on its evils.

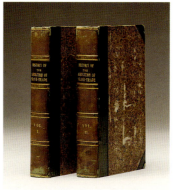

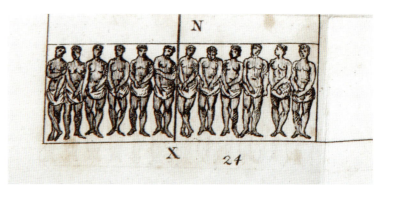

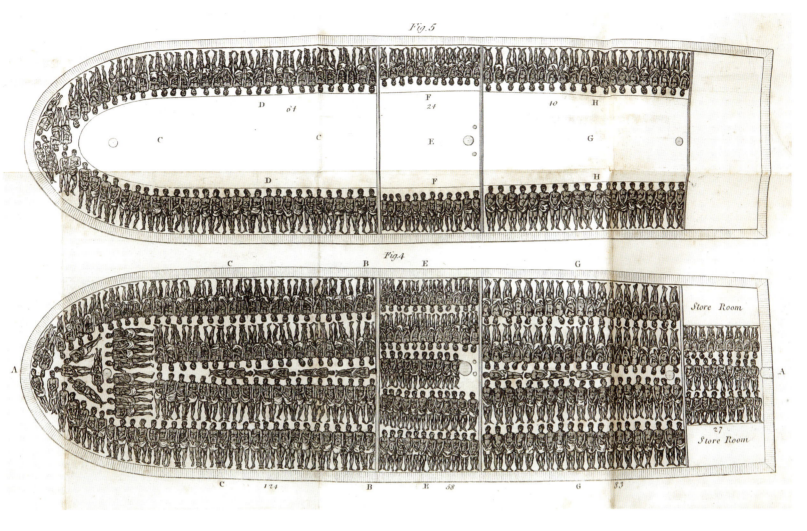

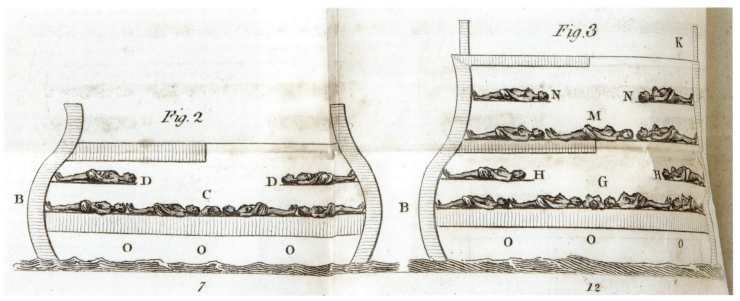

Accounts Presented to the House of Commons, 1806
William Irving, Inspector General of the Imports and Exports
of Great Britain
Printed paper
13 x 8 in.

The African slave trade was a lucrative business that sustained the power of the British Empire into the 19th century. Yet the headlong rush of British businessmen into international trade was regulated by Parliament—ironically, to ensure that the wealth garnered by the sale of black slaves was fairly shared. *Accounts Presented to the House of Commons* confirms that ships could carry well over 3.8 million slaves during a ten-year period, from 1796 to 1805— shattering the myth that during the three centuries of transatlantic slave trading, only ten to twelve million Africans were transported to the New World. In one year alone, 149 ships transported 53,021 slaves from the ports along the west coast of Africa to the British West Indies.

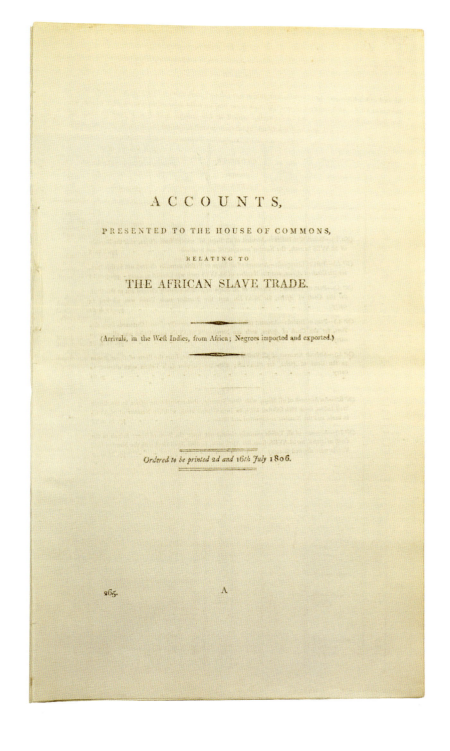

ACCOUNTS,

PRESENTED TO THE HOUSE OF COMMONS,

RELATING TO

THE AFRICAN SLAVE TRADE.

(Arrivals, in the West Indies, from Africa; Negroes imported and exported.)

Ordered to be printed 2d and 16th July 1806.

265.   A

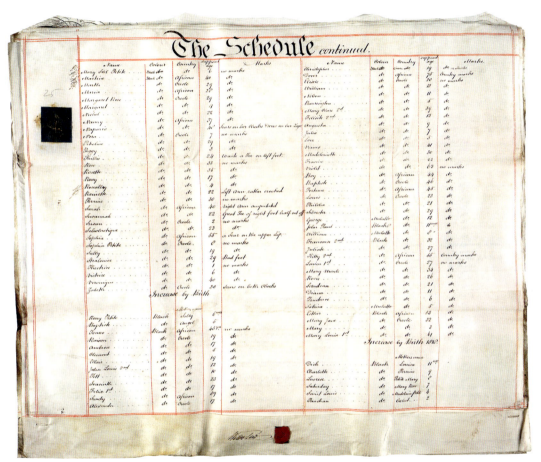

Schedule of over Five Hundred Slaves, 1820

William Law
Ink on vellum
25½ x 28½ x 3½ in.

William Law was forced to sell his estate on the island of Grenada to settle his debts. This inventory of assets, presented and signed by the Lord Mayor of London, includes a listing of slaves by name, color, country, supposed age, and defining marks. Although the estate auction took place nearly 15 years after the abolition of the slave trade in Britain, the inventory documents younger slaves born in Africa and bought by Law. The document also shows that black slaves, even infants a few months old, were regarded as property to be bred and bartered.

Bannaker's Almanack, 1796
né Benjamin Banneker
Extract from book
7 x 4 ½ x ¼ in.

Benjamin Banneker was born in Maryland in 1731 to a mulatto mother, Mary Banaky, and her former slave Robert, whom she married. Benjamin demonstrated great intellectual curiosity and by 1753 had constructed a working wooden clock that kept accurate time for over 50 years. At age 58, Banneker began the study of astronomy and was soon predicting solar and lunar eclipses. His almanacs were published annually from 1792 through 1797 and became best sellers in several states.

In 1791, Banneker served as a technical assistant in the first survey of Washington, D.C. Often referred to as the "Sable Astronomer," he was regarded as proof that African Americans were not intellectually inferior to Europeans. Banneker died in 1806 at the age of 74.

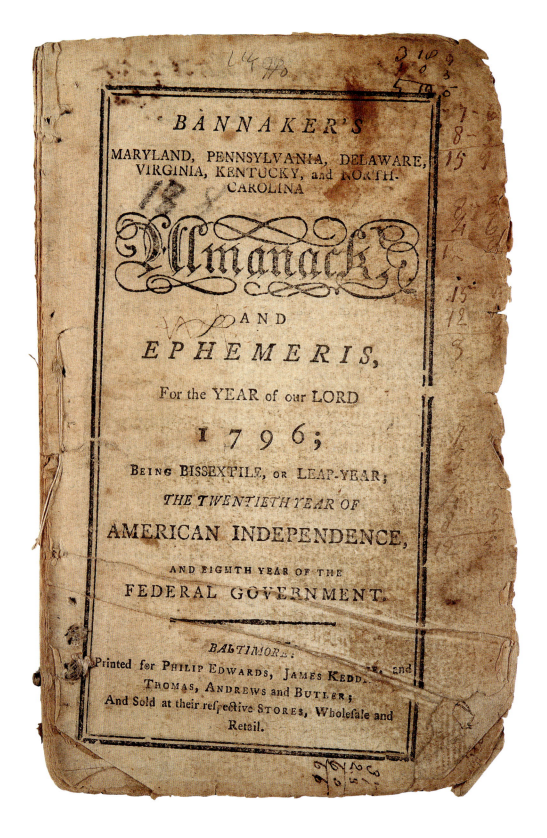

Early Genius

But in our time, as in every time, the impossible is the least that one can demand—and one is, after all, emboldened by the spectacle of human history in general, and American Negro history in particular, for it testifies to nothing less than the perpetual achievement of the impossible.

— James Baldwin

The Kinsey Collection contains remarkable examples of African American works of genius. From these, the Kinseys forged their journey as stewards, tending, educating, and cultivating the landscape of social justice to yield evidence of continued excellence.

The Kinseys endeavored to become stewards of the work of prominent early black painters who earned both recognition and financial freedom by exercising technical expertise. These artists painted portraits and landscapes, as the style of the times required. The beauty of their images demonstrates their interpretation of a tradition studied and mastered in Europe at a time when most African Americans were toiling as slaves in fields and kitchens across America.

It is important to note the role that Europe played in the complex intersections of inclusion and prejudice that shaped the lives of Africans and African Americans for centuries. Under the umbrella of European imperialism, Africans became chattel, while African American intellectual and creative talent was encouraged and valued. Many prominent Europeans supported the development of individual black artists, musicians, and scholars while ignoring the plight of brown and black people throughout the world. This trend began upon first contact in ancient times, was resurrected when the Portuguese discovered the West African coast, and continued with the French and British examples shown here. This conflicted approach to black identity would significantly affect African American cultural commodification globally, and for generations.

Porcupine's Gazette, **June 22, 1797**
William Cobbett, publisher
Printed paper
11 x 19 in.

William Cobbett began publishing this pro-British daily paper in Philadelphia. After battling with the anti-Federalist paper *Aurora* and losing a libel judgment against Benjamin Rush, the paper ceased publication in 1799.

Newspapers were used extensively to advertise for the recapture of runaway slaves. In the upper right corner of this issue is a notice that reads: "One Hundred Dollars Reward" for a runaway negro man named Abraham, placed by Thomas Marsh Forman Sassafras Neck, Cecil County, Maryland.

The 1793 Fugitive Slave Act, designated in full as "An Act respecting fugitives from justice, and persons escaping from the service of their masters," was the mechanism by which the government protected the property rights of slave owners. The government could pursue runaway slaves in any state or territory and ensure slave owners of their property rights as guaranteed in Article IV of the 1787 Constitution. The burden of proof was always on the enslaved person, to demonstrate their status as a free person. The Fugitive Slave Law therefore presumed guilt rather than innocence in the case of judicial proceedings involving black persons. This pernicious law still casts a shadow over the lives of blacks in this country, particularly the practice of racial profiling.

Note: *The New York Times* did not begin capitalizing the word "Negro" until 1922.

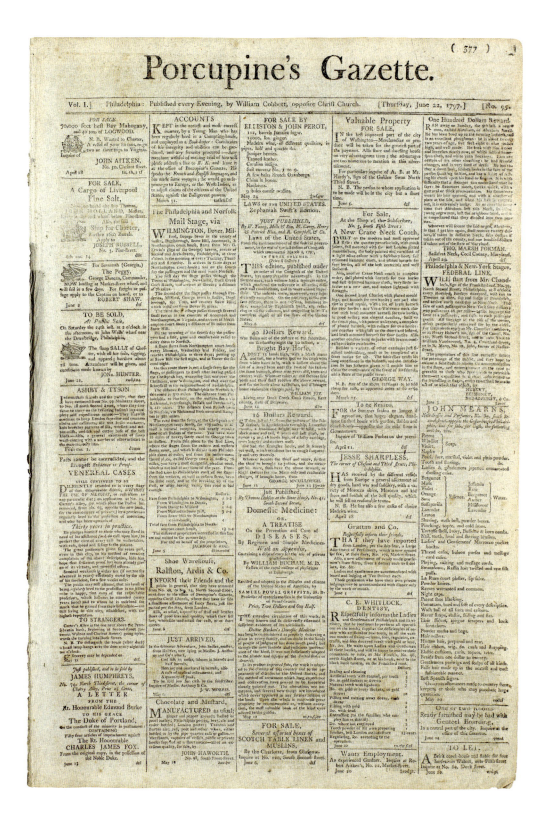

Woodblocks, from *Histoire de Napoléon* by Jacques de Norvins, 1839

Denis Auguste Marie Raffet, illustrator

Wood

4 ½ x 3 ¾ in. each

These woodblocks and their woodcut prints depict Haitian revolutionary leader Toussaint L' Ouverture dictating a letter, and a group of Dominican rebels spying on French troops in Santo Domingo during the French campaign in Cuba and Santo Domingo. L'Ouverture led slave revolts against the French and established a new constitution during his peaceful and prosperous reign over Haiti. He and his well-trained military fended off attacks from both British and Spanish invaders. He was tricked by LeClerc, a proxy of Napoleon Bonaparte, and jailed in France, where he died in 1803.

Nancy Gardener was born on September 15, 1779, in Newbury Port, Massachusetts, the granddaughter of slaves. Her father died when she was two months old; her mother suffered an emotional breakdown after she was widowed for the third time. Nancy and her siblings picked and sold berries to supplement their meager household income. Eventually, she left home and labored as a domestic servant for white families. With her marriage to Nero Prince in 1824, however, the course of her life changed dramatically. Prince was the founder of Prince Hall Free Masons in Boston. Together they traveled to St. Petersburg, Russia, and lived there for nine years, along with twenty paid black servants, at the court of the czar of Russia. Her husband worked as a footman at the court, and Nancy pursued an education, learning several languages. She established a business making fine clothing for babies and children, with the support of the empress herself. In 1833 she returned to Boston due to poor health, but her husband pre-deceased her before returning to the U.S.

In her biography, *A Narrative of the Life and Travels of Mrs. Nancy Prince*, first published in 1850, with two later editions, Prince narrates her experiences both in Russia and in the U.S. She recounts her journey from Jamaica back to Boston, during which the ship took a detour due to severe weather. The ship's captain left her stranded in New Orleans with no money, and she feared she would be seized by a slave owner. While awaiting passage to New York, she witnessed the oppression experienced by her people in the South. Prince describes her missionary work in the British-controlled West Indies, and her abolitionist work both in America and in the West Indies. She died in 1856.

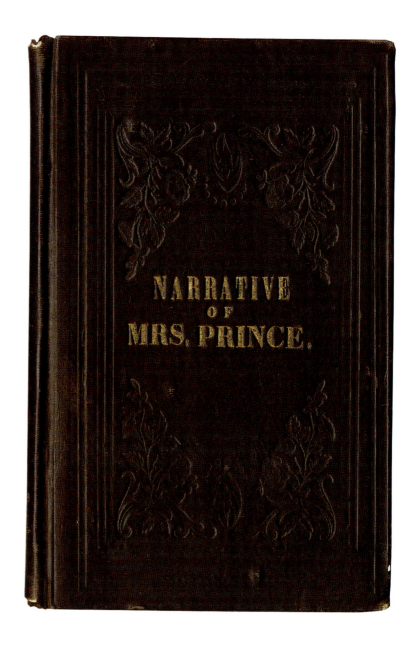

Narrative of the Life and Travels of Mrs. Nancy Prince, 1850
Nancy Prince
Book, First Edition
6 ½ x 4 ½ x ¼ in.

Landscape, Autumn, ca. 1865
Robert Scott Duncanson
Oil on board
16 ¾ x 13 ¼ in.

Lilacs, 1890
Charles Ethan Porter
Oil on canvas
21 ¾ x 18 in.

Four Cows in a Meadow, 1893
Edward Mitchell Bannister
Oil on canvas
16 ¾ x 20 ¾ in.

Mt. Tacoma from Lake Washington, ca. 1885
Grafton Tyler Brown
Oil on canvas en grisaille
22 ½ x 32 ¼ in.

Street Scene, Tangier, 1913
Henry O. Tanner
Etching
18 ¾ x 20 in.

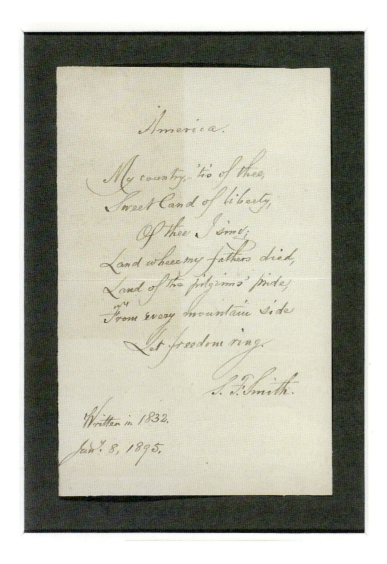

My Country 'Tis of Thee, 1895
Samuel Francis Smith
Image 7 x 4 ½ in, letter 6 x 4 in.

Smith, an American clergyman and poet, was the author of the national hymn "America" (1832), often known as "My Country 'Tis of Thee." Smith was asked by music educator Lowell Mason to translate lyrics from a German patriotic hymn. Instead, Smith wrote new lyrics for the hymn that became known as "America."

INCIDENTS

IN THE

LIFE OF A SLAVE GIRL.

WRITTEN BY HERSELF.

"Northerners know nothing at all about Slavery. They think it is perpetual bondage only. They have no conception of the depth of *degradation* involved in that word, SLAVERY; if they had, they would never cease their efforts until so horrible a system was overthrown."

A WOMAN OF NORTH CAROLINA.

"Rise up, ye women that are at ease! Hear my voice, ye careless daughters! Give ear unto my speech."

ISAIAH xxxii. 9.

EDITED BY L. MARIA CHILD.

BOSTON:
PUBLISHED FOR THE AUTHOR.
1861.

Incidents in the Life of a Slave Girl, 1861
Harriet Ann Jacobs
Book
8 x 5 ½ x 1 in.

This book was written by Harriet Jacobs (1813–1897) under the pen name Linda Brent. It describes the horrors of slavery and Jacobs' daring pursuit of freedom. Her story, mindful of the well-known diary of Anne Frank, tells a similar tale of fear and confinement. Jacobs hid from her master for seven years in a "coffin-like space" before finding a path to freedom.

The Uncalled, 1898
Paul Laurence Dunbar
Book, First Edition
8 x 5 x 1 in.

Paul Laurence Dunbar was born in Kentucky to two Kentucky natives. His mother was a former slave and his father an escaped slave who went on to serve in the 55th Massachusetts Infantry Regiment and the 5th Massachusetts Colored Calvary Regiment during the Civil War. Paul's mother instilled in her children a love for storytelling and literature. By the age of 6, Paul had written his first poem, and by the age of 9, he gave his first reading. His mother separated from his father and supported her poverty-stricken family by doing domestic work for white families, one of them the family of Orville and Wilbur Wright. The only African American student in his class, Paul attended school with the Wright brothers. He became the editor of the school newspaper, president of the school literary society, and class president. With the help of the Wright brothers, Paul published an African American newsletter in Dayton called *The Tattler*. He went on to publish his first collection of poetry, *Oak and Ivy*, in 1893, paying off his debt to his publisher by working as an elevator operator.

His second book, *Majors and Minors*, published in 1895 in both standard English and black dialect, brought him national fame. Paul traveled to London to give readings of his work, and on his return in 1898, married Alice Ruth Moore. They created companion poetry books. Paul took a job at the Library of Congress, but had to resign due to ill health, which led to depression and heavy drinking. He nonetheless produced twelve books of poetry, four of short stories, a play, and five novels. He died in 1906 at only 33.

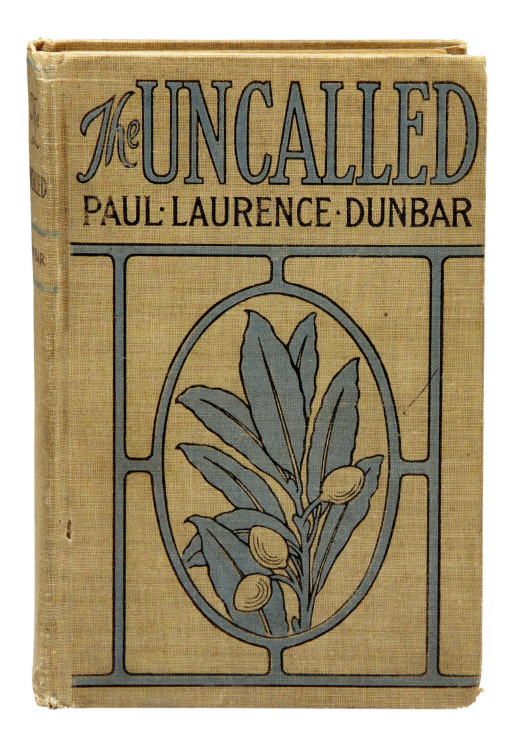

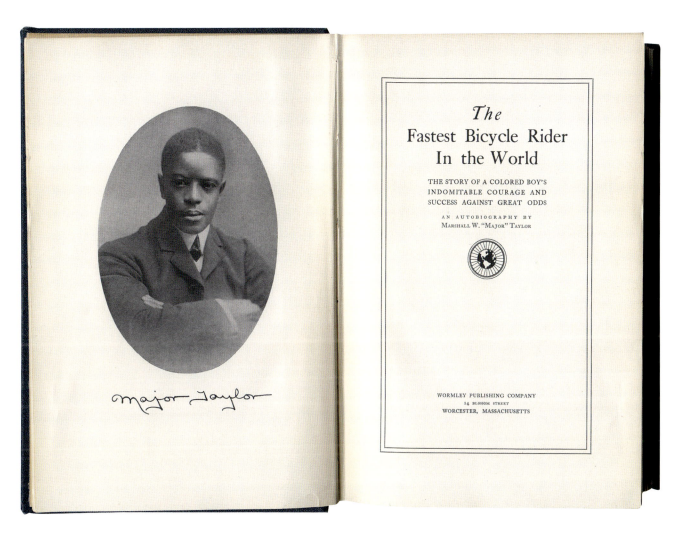

The Fastest Bicycle Rider In the World, 1928
Marshall W. "Major" Taylor
Book, First Edition
9 x 6 ¼ x 1 in.

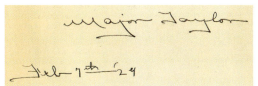

Marshall Walter Taylor (1878–1932) was an American cyclist who set several world records and then won the world one-mile track cycling championship in 1899. He was the first African American athlete to achieve the level of world champion in the sport, and only the second black man to win any world championship, after the Canadian boxer George Dixon.

Taylor grew up with a well-to-do white family that his father worked for as a coachman, where he was treated like a member of the family. They gave young Taylor a Safety bicycle, which became his ticket to fame and fortune. Banned from racing in his home state of Indiana, he moved to the East Coast, where he turned professional. In 1903 he competed in Europe and was victorious in 40 of 57 races. When he retired in 1910 at only 32, he said it was because he could no longer tolerate the racism.

Female slave shackles, ca. 1850

Maker unknown

Iron

14 ¼ x 21 ½ x 3 in.

Slavery

In every human breast, God has implanted a principle which we call love of freedom; it is impatient of oppression and pants for deliverance.

— Phillis Wheatley

For over 258 years, American slavery was a harsh reality for the majority of the African Americans living in the United States. While many whites served as indentured servants in the colonies, they were able to work off their servitude after a number of years. Black slaves and their progeny had no such recourse. The Kinseys have amassed formidable evidence of the scope of slavery in a nation founded on liberty.

Slavery is often seen as an incomprehensible part of American culture, to the point that many refuse to or simply cannot discuss it. Thomas Jefferson acknowledged the misery of black slaves, and even mused in *Notes of the State of Virginia* (1781) that the risk of emancipation was the "ten thousand recollections … of the injuries [blacks] have sustained." This understanding did not stop him from fathering and freeing his children by his slave, Sally Hemings, but did express his conflicted feelings on the abolition of slavery.

The dichotomy of African American identity is written large in the life of Frederick Douglass. Born a slave in Maryland in 1818, Douglass escaped from his owner to travel to New York and onward to become the pre-eminent African American spokesman for abolition. In Massachusetts he met abolitionist leader William Lloyd Garrison, who encouraged him to become active in the movement. Before he was 30, Douglass had become an accomplished orator and writer, lecturing throughout the world and advocating for the equality of all people.

Douglass' story inspires all audiences to recognize that vast potential lies in the minds of all individuals, who can achieve greatness if given the opportunity. His message changed the lives of his own people, but it also reached those who may not have realized their complicity in the subjugation of others. Douglass' English audiences were so swayed by his words that they bought his freedom for 700 pounds, securing his ability to spread his message.

The Kinseys are drawn to these ambiguities, stumbling blocks between compassion and complacency. They collect provocative ephemera as evidence that things are never simple or absolute. In these intersections, the Kinseys seek the vestiges of slavery that document African American endurance. Whether delivering silent resistance or booming oratory on the evils of slavery, blacks survived and thrived.

"Any Person May Kill and Destroy Said Slaves," 1798

Arrest Proclamation for Jem and Mat, escaped slaves issued by Warren County, NC

Ink on paper

19 x 17 ¼ in.

This arrest proclamation for two escaped slaves, issued by the state of North Carolina, amounted to a death sentence. Were they able to escape to the North, however, they would still have been in jeopardy: Article 4 of the U.S. Constitution required that runaway slaves had to be returned to their masters, and a measure signed by George Washington in 1793, "An act respecting fugitives from justice, and persons escaping from the service of their masters" —usually referred to as the Fugitive Slave Law—made it a federal crime to assist an escaped slave. In 1842, the U.S. Supreme Court weakened this provision, ruling that state governments need not assist in repatriating slaves to their Southern masters. But the Fugitive Slave Act of 1850 superseded that ruling, fining any federal marshall who did not arrest an escaped slave (and rewarding officials who did). Blacks so detained had no legal recourse.

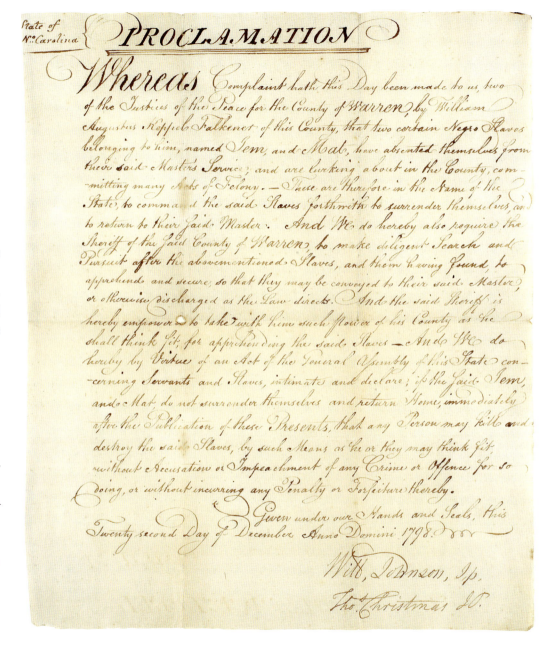

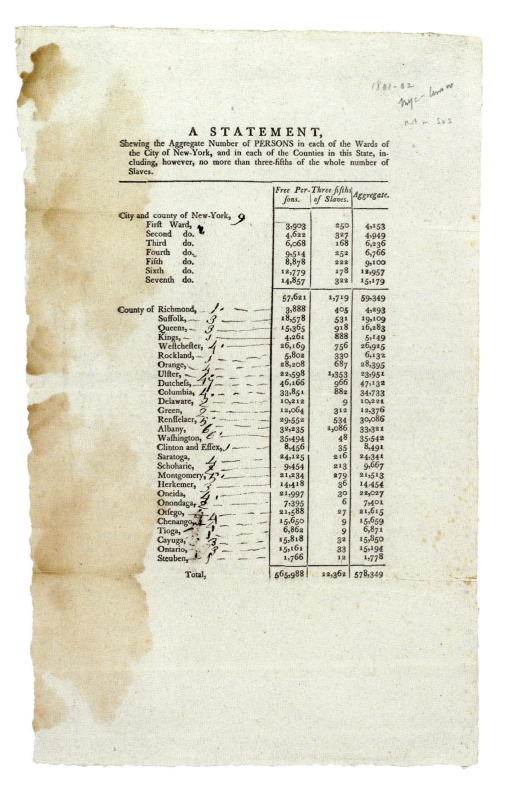

A STATEMENT,

Shewing the Aggregate Number of PERSONS in each of the Wards of the City of New-York, and in each of the Counties in this State, including, however, no more than three-fifths of the whole number of Slaves.

	Free Persons.	Three fifths of Slaves.	Aggregate.
City and county of New-York,			
First Ward,	3,903	250	4,153
Second do.	4,622	327	4,949
Third do.	6,068	168	6,236
Fourth do.	9,514	252	6,766
Fifth do.	8,878	222	9,100
Sixth do.	12,779	178	12,957
Seventh do.	14,857	322	15,179
	57,621	1,719	59,349
County of Richmond,	3,888	405	4,293
Suffolk,	18,578	531	19,109
Queens,	15,365	918	16,283
Kings,	4,261	888	5,149
Westchester,	26,169	756	26,925
Rockland,	5,802	330	6,132
Orange,	28,208	687	28,395
Ulster,	22,598	1,353	23,951
Dutchess,	46,166	966	47,132
Columbia,	33,851	882	34,733
Delaware,	10,212	9	10,221
Green,	12,064	312	12,376
Rensselaer,	29,552	534	30,086
Albany,	32,235	1,086	33,321
Washington,	35,494	48	35,542
Clinton and Essex,	8,456	35	8,491
Saratoga,	24,125	216	24,341
Schoharie,	9,454	213	9,667
Montgomery,	21,234	279	21,513
Herkemer,	14,418	36	14,454
Oneida,	21,997	30	22,027
Onondaga,	7,395	6	7,401
Otsego,	21,588	27	21,615
Chenango,	15,650	9	15,659
Tioga,	6,862	9	6,871
Cayuga,	15,818	32	15,850
Ontario,	15,161	33	15,194
Steuben,	1,766	12	1,778
Total,	565,988	12,362	578,349

New York Census, 1801
State of New York
Printed paper
8 ¾ x 5 ¾ in.

According to the 1787 Philadelphia Convention and the compromise between Northern and Southern states, slaves were to be counted in the census as three-fifths of a person. The compromise, which was reached in the effort to unite the Northern and Southern states, was reflected in the Constitution in Article 1, demonstrating that slavery was codified in the country's foundational documents. The compromise gave the white voters of the South a disproportionately larger political voice than their counterparts in the North—though the white population of the Southern states was some 50 percent smaller.

The first U.S. census took place in 1790. This document shows the "three-fifths compromise" taking effect in the New York state census of 1801.

Handwritten slave document, 1832

William Johnson

Ink on paper

15 ½ x 10 ½ in.

This 1832 bill of sale was for William Johnson, a slave sold for $550, the equivalent of $14,000 today.

Given to Bernard and Shirley Kinsey as a gift, this document was one of the first to be included in their collection. It inspired Bernard's quest to discover both his personal history and African American historical documentation.

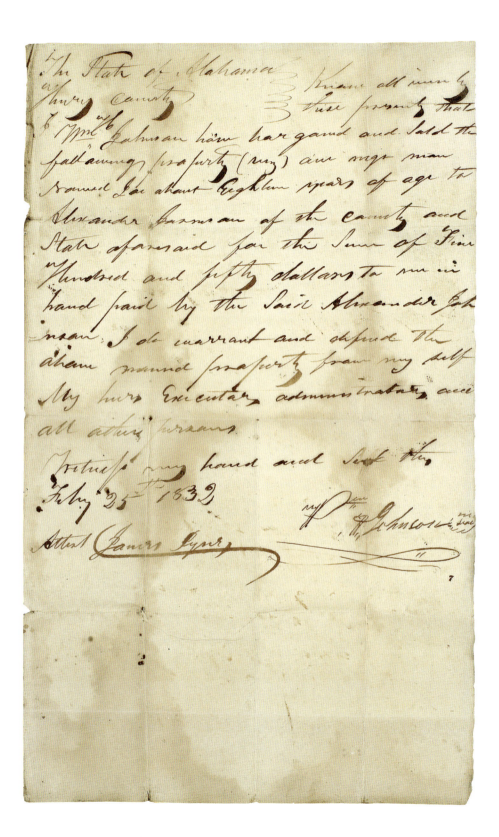

Henry Butler buys the freedom of his wife and four children for $100, 1839

Henry Butler
Ink on paper
9 x 14 ½ in.

During this period, healthy and child-bearing slaves often sold for as much as $1,800. Mary Ann Graham sold Henry Butler his family at a significant loss. This letter is extremely important to the Kinseys because it shows the compassion of the female slave owner. It offers a glimpse of humane conduct in an otherwise inhumane time.

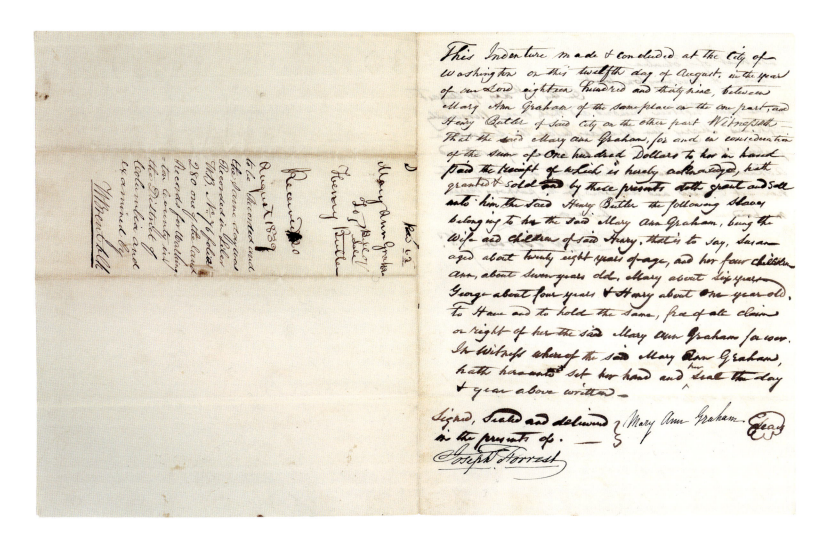

Doc. No 225: Negroes &c. Captured from Indians in Florida, 1839

J. R. Poinsett, Secretary of War

Book

9 ¼ x 5 ¾ x 1 ½ in.

This official publication was generated as a result of the campaigns of 1837–38 in Florida. President Jackson spent $15 million appropriating slaves from the Seminoles and sending them to Leon and Gasden Counties, which had the largest slave holdings in all of Florida. The legacy of slavery in these counties is still evident to Bernard and Shirley Kinsey, as Floridians and American citizens.

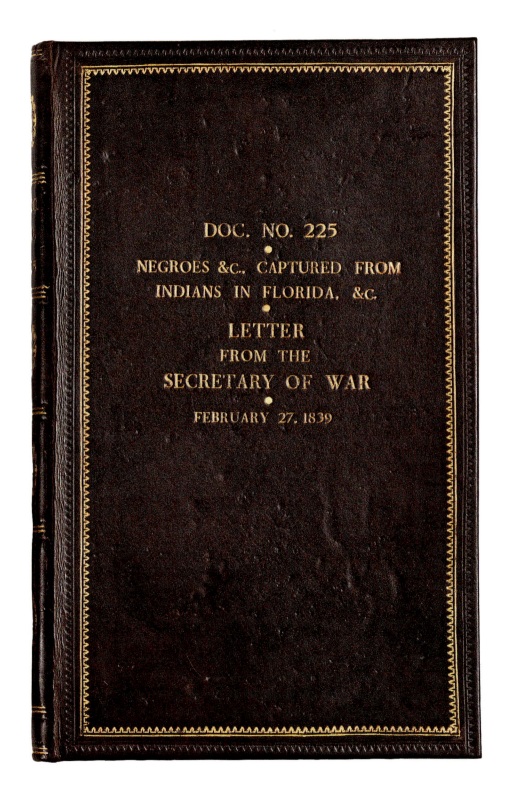

DOC. NO. 225

NEGROES &c., CAPTURED FROM
INDIANS IN FLORIDA, &c.

LETTER
FROM THE
SECRETARY OF WAR

FEBRUARY 27, 1839

Slave Tags, 1841, 1862
Metal; copper
1 ½ x 1 ½ in., each

According to the first U.S. Census in 1790, Charleston, South Carolina, was the fourth largest city in the newly formed United States. It was also the city where the most Africans were transported into the country to become enslaved people. As such, Charleston developed a sophisticated culture and economy supported by enslaved labor.

Slave badges, commonly referred to today as slave tags, were codified and came into use around 1800 only in the Charleston area to formalize a slave-hire system. After paying the city's annual license fee, an owner was issued a slave badge stamped with a number for a specific slave with a named skill. This badge had to be worn at all times by the enslaved person, and allowed the owner to hire the enslaved person out to others. Frequently a portion of the wages obtained were split with the enslaved person. With a slave badge, an enslaved person could also legally work after hours or on free time to garner additional personal income.

The practice of slaves for hire was controversial with poorer whites competing for work. Enslaved people working for hire without a badge could be heavily fined and most often punished with 20 or more lashes. .

As these badges were re-issued annually, they were disposed of regularly, and few remain in existence today. Most have been found by treasure hunters with metal detectors and are highly sought after by collectors of slave ephemera.

This document from 1857 is the original printing of the opinions and the votes of each justice of the Supreme Court of the United States in the Dred Scott case.

Dred Scott (1799 – September 17, 1858) was an African American slave who sued unsuccessfully for his freedom in the infamous Dred Scott v. Sandford case of 1857. Although he and his wife, Harriet, were slaves, the premise of the suit was that he had lived with his master, Dr. John Emerson, in Illinois and Minnesota (then part of the Wisconsin Territory), where both state laws and the Northwest Ordinance of 1787 had made slavery illegal. The Supreme Court ruled seven to two against Scott.

Chief Justice Taney's court made two sweeping rulings. The first was that Dred Scott had no right to sue in federal court because neither slaves nor free blacks were citizens of the United States. At the time the Constitution was adopted, the chief justice wrote, blacks had been "regarded as beings of an inferior order" with "no rights which the white man was bound to respect." Second, Taney declared that Congress had no right to exclude slavery from the federal territories since the Fifth Amendment prohibited seizure of property without due process. Taney himself was the second-largest slaveholder in Virginia and should have recused himself from deliberations.

For the first time since Marbury v. Madison in 1803, the Supreme Court declared an act of Congress unconstitutional. And its advocacy of this extreme pro-slavery position accelerated the start of the Civil War.

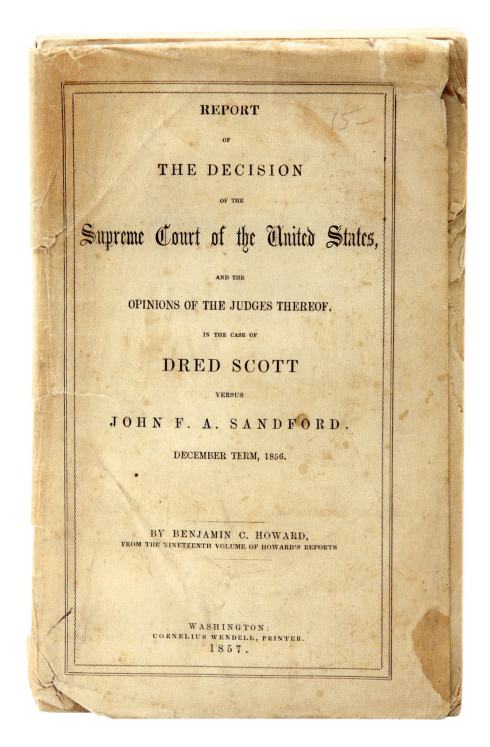

Supreme Court of the United States:
Dred Scott Decision, 1857
Printed paper
5 ½ x 9 x ½ in.

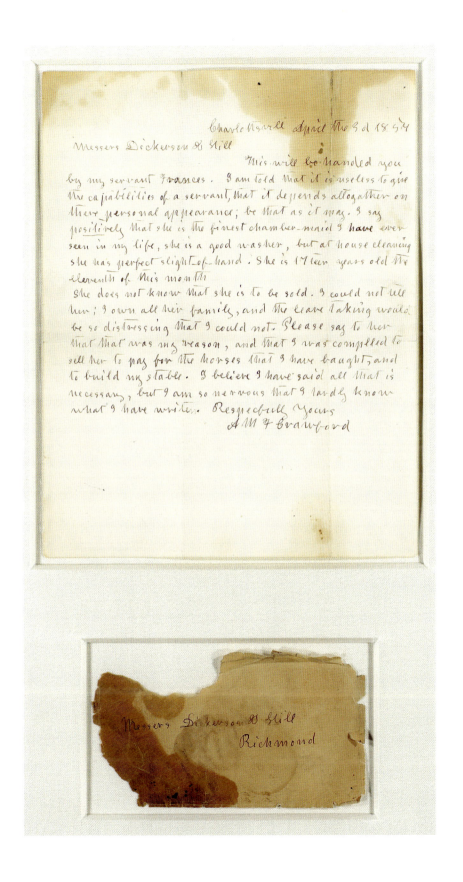

A slave carrying her fate in her hands, 1854
A. M. F. Crawford
Printed paper
19 ¾ x 12 ½ in.

This letter documents the commodification of blacks in stark terms. Frances, the young girl carrying her fate in her hands but helpless to change it, is being sold away from her family so that her owner can use the proceeds for other purchases. The owner, meanwhile, though aware of Frances' abilities and value, is entirely concerned with her own economic and emotional circumstances:

"This will be handed you by my servant Frances. I am told that it is useless to give the capabilities of a servant, that it depends alto-gather [*sic*] on there [*sic*] personal appearance; be that as it may. I say positively that she is the finest chamber-maid I have ever seen in my life, she is a good washer, but at house cleaning she has perfect slight of hand. She is 17teen [*sic*] years old the eleventh of this month.

"She does not know that she is to be sold, I couldn't tell her; I own all her family and the leave-taking would be so distressing that I could not. Please say to her that that was my reason, and that I was compelled to sell her to pay for the horses that I have bought, and to build my stable. I believe I have said all that is necessary, but I am so nervous that I hardly know what I have written. Respectfully Yours AMF Crawford"

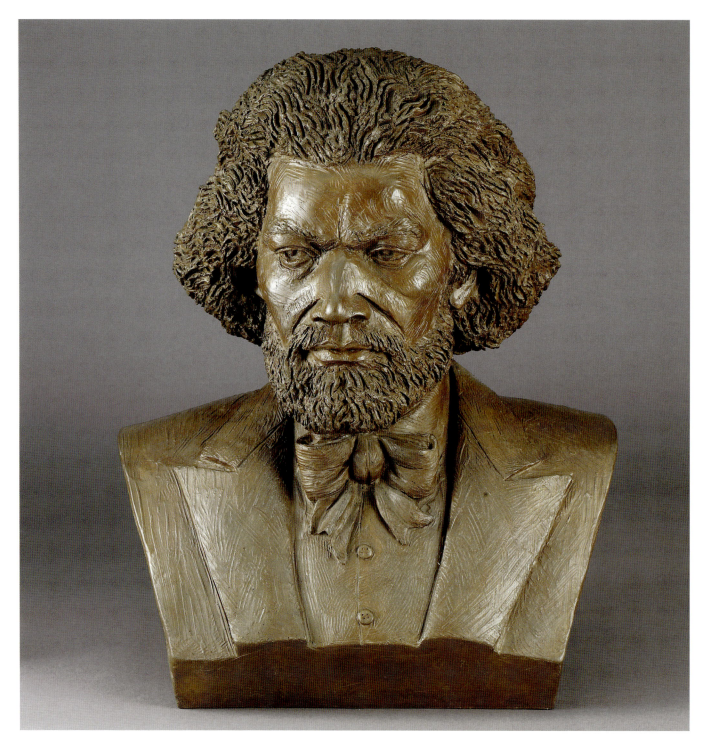

Frederick Douglass, 2003
Tina Allen
Bronze
23 x 17 ¼ x 12 in.

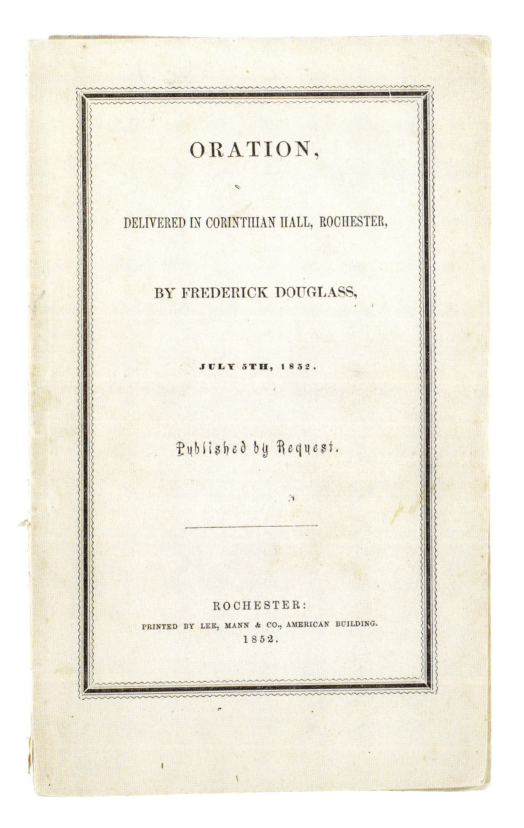

ORATION,

DELIVERED IN CORINTHIAN HALL, ROCHESTER,

BY FREDERICK DOUGLASS,

JULY 5TH, 1852.

Published by Request.

ROCHESTER:
PRINTED BY LEE, MANN & CO., AMERICAN BUILDING.
1852.

Oration Delivered in Corinthian Hall Rochester, 1852
Frederick Douglass
Pamphlet
10 ¼ x 7 x 1 ¼ in.

Frederick Douglass demonstrated his commitment to the pursuit of freedom while challenging America's celebration of liberty in a speech to the Rochester Ladies Anti-Slavery Society: "What have I, or those I represent, to do with your national independence? … This Fourth of July is yours, not mine. You may rejoice, I must mourn."

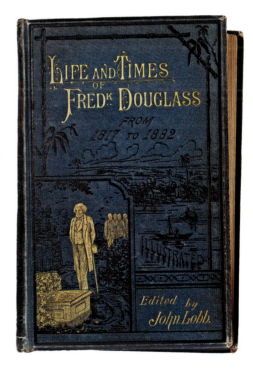

The Life and Times of Frederick Douglass from 1817 to 1832, 1882
Frederick Douglass
Book
8 ½ x 6 ½ x 1 ¾ in.

Slave Insurance, ca. 1859
Albemarle Insurance Company
Printed paper
9 ¾ x 8 in.

Slaves were a valuable commodity to their owners, and like all assets they were insured. Frances, the young slave referred to in the letter on the previous page, was most likely insured by the Albemarle Company, located in the same county as her master's plantation.

SLAVE INSURANCE!

Albemarle Insurance Company,

KNOWLES & WALFORD, Agents.

RATES OF PREMIUM FOR ONE YEAR ON $100.

AGE.	RATES.	AGE.	RATES.	AGE.	RATES.
8 to 15 years,	$1 30	31 years,	$1 62	46 years,	$2 45
16 "	1 35	32 "	1 65	47 "	2 57
17 "	1 35	33 "	1 70	48 "	2 70
18 "	1 36	34 "	1 73	49 "	2 85
19 "	1 37	35 "	1 77	50 "	3 00
20 "	1 28	36 "	1 80	51 "	3 21
21 "	1 39	37 "	1 85	52 "	3 41
22 "	1 41	38 "	1 88	53 "	3 62
23 "	1 44	39 "	1 92	54 "	3 86
24 "	1 45	40 "	1 97	55 "	4 16
25 "	1 47	41 "	2 00	56 "	4 50
26 "	1 50	42 "	2 07	57 "	4 85
27 "	1 52	43 "	2 15	58 "	5 00
28 "	1 55	44 "	2 22	59 "	5 33
29 "	1 58	45 "	2 33	60 "	5 66
30 "	1 59				

Rates for $100, with privilege of Renewing the Policy 2, 3 or 4 years, without further Examination or Increase of Rates.

AGE.	RATES.	AGE.	RATES.
14 to 19 years,	$1 50	35 to 39 years,	$2 50
20 to 24 "	1 75	40 to 44 "	2 75
25 to 29 "	2 00	45 to 50 "	3 00
30 to 34 "	2 25		

Dr. F. W. HANCOCK,   -   -   -   Medical Examiner.

N. B.—Office, No. 21 Pearl Street. January next (1860) we shall remove to the store occupied by C. D. YALE & Co., No. 130 MAIN STREET, a few doors above Governor Street.   KNOWLES & WALFORD.

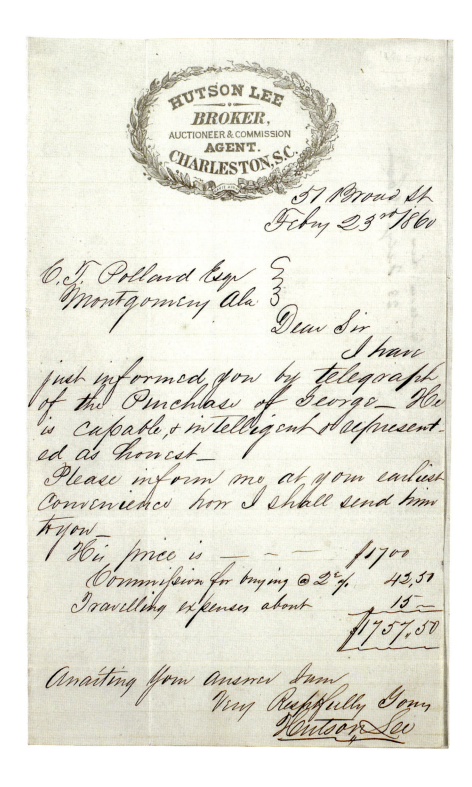

A Letter from Hutson Lee to C. T. Pollard, Esq.,1860
Hutson Lee
Ink on paper
8 ¼ x 5 in.

This letter documents the profitable business of trading slaves. It includes sale price, commission, and delivery fees.

"Mammy of Ye Olden Times," ca. 1860
Rare Large Format Albumen Photograph
10 x 15 in.

This photograph shows an enslaved older black woman sitting on the porch next to a small basket, with a set of keys attached to her coat. She probably worked inside the house. Inscribed by hand with the title "Mammy of Ye Olden Times."

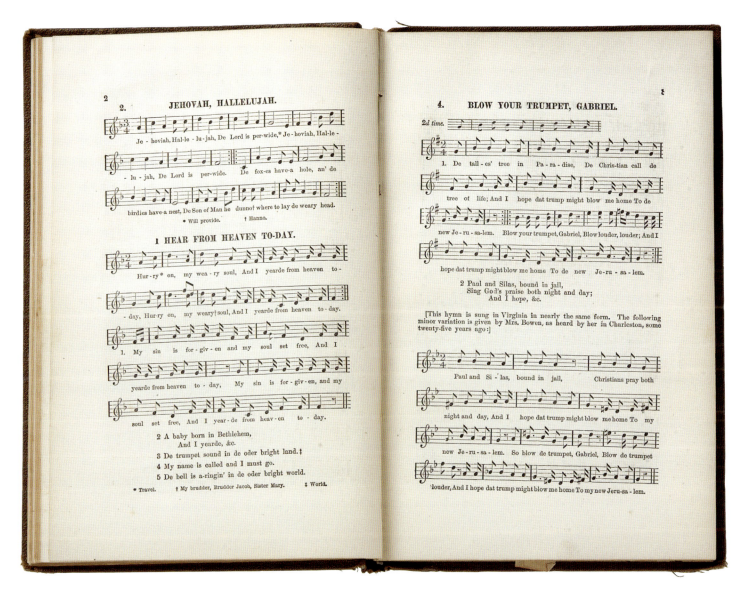

Slave Songs, 1867

A. Simpson & Co.

Book

6 ¼ x 9 ¼ x ¾ in.

Published shortly after slavery was abolished in the United States, this book was intended to record and preserve the songs of enslaved people at the time of their freedom. Most of the songs are primarily religious in nature.

Lyrics such as "going to the promised land," however, had connotations that were powerfully linked to the hardships of enslaved people.

Slave songs had important cultural roles that extended into the future. Music and song were a significant element of the various African cultures that were forcibly migrated to the Americas. Gospel music, the blues, and jazz are among the descendants of the slave song.

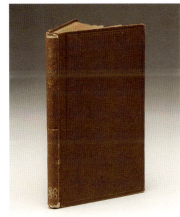

***Revolutionary Soldier,* 1994**
Ed Dwight
Bronze
15 ½ x 12 ½ x 6 in.

Crispus Attucks is remembered as the first American to die in the Boston Massacre of 1770. It is thought that Attucks was an escaped slave of African and Native American descent. In John Adams' defense of the British soldiers who committed the massacre, he described the crowd as "a motley rabble of saucy boys, negroes and molattoes, Irish teagues and outlandish jack tarrs." Despite negative categorizations and daily discrimination, African Americans' desire to find freedom led them to fight side-by-side with those who would further oppress them. Thousands of African Americans died in the battles of the Revolution.

African Americans and War

I never saw such fighting as was done by the Negro regiment…The question that negroes will fight is settled; besides they make better solders in every respect than any troops I have ever had under my command.

— General James Blunt

African Americans are no strangers to war. Black men have voluntarily fought in every major battle on American soil, primarily for the cause of American liberty, despite the continuing disenfranchisement of black people.

The idea that black people would give the ultimate sacrifice for freedom to a country that did not recognize them as human beings fascinates Bernard Kinsey. It both perplexes him and resonates with his own mission to inspire and educate, in the face of the contradictory rhetoric and discriminatory practices affecting so many people of color.

So often, the altruistic acts of bravery demonstrated by black men and women, particularly during times of war, are omitted from the annals of history. This became a powerful motivation for the Kinseys to collect examples of these moments of courage and selflessness. Of special interest is black participation in the Civil War, when the United States was faced with a cultural crisis, with black people at its center, that tore the nation apart.

For over half a century before the Civil War, slavery was a highly contested, morally problematic issue for America. A country founded on freedom grew prosperous on the back of a brutal labor system that considered blacks only slightly above livestock. While many opposed slavery in theory, the practice was deeply entrenched as an American prerogative, exercised by ten of the first fifteen presidents as well as land owners who had a financial stake in the national and global commercial marketplace.

Although Europe had instituted the transatlantic slave trade to expand its global power and reap riches from abroad, it struggled to end the practice in the name of morality. In 1807, the British Parliament passed "An Act for the Abolition of the Slave Trade," which decisively ceased legal slave trading in western Europe, and in January 1808, a similar measure was to take effect in the United States. Slavery was not completely abolished in England and all of her colonies, however, until 1833, and it took until 1860 to convince African kings and European pirates and raiders to stop the now illegal slave trade. It took much more to end slavery in the United States.

Only an act of war could convince white slave owners to release their claim of property on millions of African Americans in bondage. The first act of rebellion was the declared secession of seven Southern states in 1860, before Abraham Lincoln became president. In 1862,

Lincoln signed the Emancipation Proclamation, declaring an official end to slavery and forcing England, which initially supported the South, to step aside. Lincoln called on the Union states to amass a volunteer army, and free black men enlisted in large numbers to support the liberation of their brethren in the South. Black slaves faced double jeopardy, as many plantation owners vowed to kill their slaves before seeing them free. Many slaves fled and joined the ranks of the Northern free men fighting for the Union. Over 180,000 African American soldiers fought in the Civil War. They earned lower wages and had to pay further monies for their accommodations, and they fought and died at a higher rate than their counterparts for the ideal of freedom. Twenty-five African Americans were awarded the Medal of Honor for their service during the Civil War.

Emancipation Proclamation, 1862

Abraham Lincoln

Printed paper

7 x 4 ¾ in.

Lincoln issued two Emancipation Proclamations in 1862–63; the copy shown here is of the first. Both were executive orders, issued first to the military, who were to enforce them. The first proclamation, issued September 22, granted freedom to all slaves in the Confederacy; if the Southern states returned to the Union by January 1 of the following year, however, it was not to take effect. The second proclamation, issued January 1, named the ten seceding states in which slaves were now to be freed (with exceptions too detailed to list here).

Neither measure abolished slavery in the North or in border states that had not seceded, such as Missouri, Kentucky, Maryland, or Delaware. Only about 20,000 slaves were freed in 1863, in areas of the South controlled by Union soldiers. Slavery was made illegal throughout the United States when the 13th Amendment to the Constitution was passed in 1865. About four million slaves were ultimately freed.

GENERAL ORDERS, }   WAR DEPARTMENT,
No. 139.   ADJUTANT GENERAL'S OFFICE,
     Washington, Sept. 24, 1862.

The following Proclamation by the President is published for the information and government of the Army and all concerned:

BY THE PRESIDENT OF THE UNITED STATES OF AMERICA.

A PROCLAMATION.

I, ABRAHAM LINCOLN, President of the United States of America, and Commander-in-Chief of the Army and Navy thereof, do hereby proclaim and declare that hereafter, as heretofore, the war will be prosecuted for the object of practically restoring the constitutional relation between the United States and each of the States, and the people thereof, in which States that relation is or may be suspended or disturbed.

That it is my purpose, upon the next meeting of Congress, to again recommend the adoption of a practical measure tendering pecuniary aid to the free acceptance or rejection of all Slave States, so called, the people whereof may not then be in rebellion against the United States, and which States may then have voluntarily adopted, or thereafter may voluntarily adopt, immediate or gradual abolishment of slavery within their respective limits; and that the effort to colonize persons of African descent, with their consent, upon this continent or elsewhere, with the previously obtained consent of the governments existing there, will be continued.

That on the first day of January, in the year of our Lord one thousand eight hundred and sixty-three, all persons held as slaves within any State or designated part of a State, the people whereof shall then be in rebellion against the United States, shall be then, thenceforward, and forever free; and the Executive Government of the United States, including the military and naval authority thereof, will recognise and maintain the freedom of such persons, and will do no act or acts to repress such persons, or any of them, in any efforts they may make for their actual freedom.

That the Executive will, on the first day of January aforesaid, by proclamation, designate the States, and parts of States, if any, in which the people thereof respectively shall then be in rebellion against

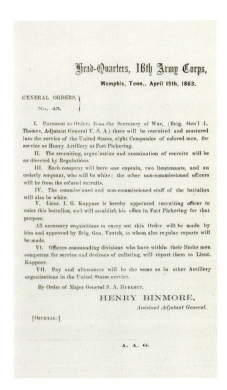

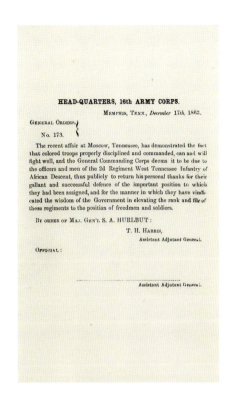

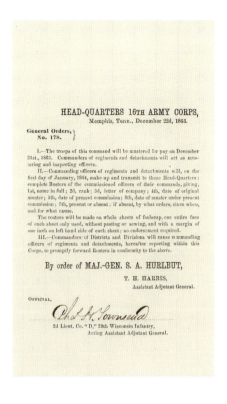

16th Army Corps General Orders No. 45
Major General S. A. Hurlbut
Printed paper
7 x 4 in.

16th Army Corps General Orders No. 173
Major General S. A. Hurlbut
Printed paper
7 x 4 in.

16th Army Corps General Orders No. 178
Major General S. A. Hurlbut
Printed paper
7 x 4 in.

The decision to allow black participation in the Union Army was a contentious one. Following the establishment of the Bureau of Colored Troops, general orders were issued detailing the recruitment, formation, and commendation of colored regiments under white commissioned officers.

COME AND JOIN US BROTHERS.
PUBLISHED BY THE SUPERVISORY COMMITTEE FOR RECRUITING COLORED REGIMENTS
1210 CHESTNUT ST. PHILADELPHIA.

United States Soldiers at Camp William Penn, 1863
Supervisory Committee for Recruiting Colored Regiments
Chromolithograph print
22 ½ x 25 in.

Blacks were banned from military combat until late 1862, despite pleas and petitions demanding inclusion in the war effort. Once the ban was lifted, black leaders including Frederick Douglass encouraged blacks to join the fight. The Bureau of Colored Troops was formed to recruit and register black volunteers for the Union Army.

Roughly 180,000 blacks served as Union soldiers during the Civil War. Following the Emancipation Proclamation, black troops were allowed to fight as Union soldiers. This is one of the first recruiting posters used to promote black service.

PRESENTATION OF COLORS TO THE TWENTIETH UNITED STATES COLORED INFANTRY, COLONEL BERTRAM, IN NEW YORK CITY, MARCH 5TH, 1864.

THE SOLDIER IN OUR CIVIL WAR.

***Presentation of Colors to the Twentieth United
States Colored Infantry, March 5, 1864***

Harper's Weekly
Book plate etching
16 ¾ x 21 ½ in.

Blacks who served in the military in this period were rarely officers, and few photographs remain to document their contributions. It is estimated that as many as 5,000 blacks fought for the Confederacy.

Civil War Black Corporal from Confederate New Orleans, ca. 1860
Carte de visite
2 ½ x 4 in.

Portrait of African American, Private Nelson J. Campbell of the Sixth U. S. Colored Calvary, ca. 1860
Carte de visite
2 ½ x 4 in.

"According to the revised official data, of the slightly over two million troops in the United States Volunteers, over 316,000 died (from all causes), or 15.2%. Of the 67,000 Regular Army (white) troops, 8.6%, or not quite 6,000, died. Of the approximately 180,000 United States Colored Troops, however, over 36,000 died, or 20.5%. In other words, the mortality rate amongst the United States Colored Troops in the Civil War was 35% greater than that among other troops, notwithstanding the fact that the former were not enrolled until some eighteen months after the fighting began" (Herbert Aptheker, *Negro Casualties in the Civil War*).

Letter recounting the murder of slaves, 1862

Union soldier

Ink on paper

12 ½ x 8 in.

"Things as they are …" A letter written by a Union soldier reports the murder of four slaves by their master. The soldier writes to his father:

"On the 3rd day of this month [November] we of the fourth Division took up a line of march for some point south of this place [Bolivar, Tenn.] supposed to be Holly Springs. We moved about eight miles in the morning. Marched some ten or twelve miles that day and camped for the night being deprived of only six teams to the Regt, we were forced to leave the most of our camp equipage behind. Also knapsacks carrying our blankets across our shoulders, and haversack with three days rations which left us destitute of many of the necessities of a soldier. The weather being somewhat colder than we would have desired and like all other armies (when on like marches) as soon as we broke ranks some went to cooking while others started after Straw and something to eat such as sweet potatoes & fresh pork while others would go through the different plantations rob and plunder. Well, as I stated previously we had camped for the night and one of these squads had gone across the country to a plantation (within sight) after something for his supper. On entering the house he found it deserted but the stove was not cold yet so he being anxious to know all about the matter started for the Negro huts and what did he behold! The boddies [sic] of four Negroes, two male and two female the former were hung by the necks and the latter were beaten to death with a club. After a short visit he returned with his comrades to camp and reported the fact. Some Negroes were sent to bury them and on their way when they met another the fifth one and he the only survivor to tell the tale which was as follows: This Negro was cut across his throat until when he went to drink the water ran down the outside of his throat. I saw this with my own eyes and defy anyone to deny it. His testimony was that on the approach of our army his master … told the three Negro men & two women to run to the woods and not let the D----d Yankee cusses to see them, for if they did they would shoot them all, which they refused to do. And he took to the club, thinking to scare them by hitting one of the wenches which he done over the head. He carrying a Bowie knife like all others of his class. The three men piched [sic] at him to protect their wives and he struck the first, after which left and saw the overseer enter the house from the cotton gin. He saw no more of the fracas until he returned with some of our boys and there found his wife dead. Also the two others. The fact was made known and his house was burned to the ground and property all confiscated and [illegible]."

Union soldier, ca. 1864

Maker unknown

Hand-colored tintype

3 ¾ x 3 ¼ x ¾ in.

9th Cavalry Buffalo Soldiers, Parade Flag, ca. 1889
Maker unknown
Fabric
22 ½ x 32 ½ in.

In 1866, General Phillip Sheridan was authorized to raise one regiment of "colored" cavalry, former Union soldiers, to be designated as the 9th Regiment. The "Buffalo Soldiers" served with distinction, from patrolling frontier towns acting as militia to fighting in direct combat. Six officers and thirteen enlisted men in the 9th Regiment earned the Medal of Honor during the Plains Indians Wars of the late 1860s. Another five medals were awarded during the Spanish American War, including recognition of valor at the battle of San Juan Hill.

Young Boy, ca. 1900
Maker unknown
Hand-colored silver print
12 x 18 in.

Hearts and Souls

"I am an invisible man... of substance, of flesh and bone, fiber and liquid – and I might even be said to possess a mind. I am invisible, understand, simply because people refuse to see me."
— Ralph Ellison
from the *Invisible Man*

The period from 1875 to 1910 saw enormous change in America. America's population doubled in a single generation, from 1875 to 1900. Black Congressmen and Senators were elected to the 41st and 42nd Congresses and were instrumental in passing the 1875 Civil Rights Bill, which guaranteed equal access to public accommodations, including inns, transportation, and entertainment venues. The 1883 ruling by the Supreme Court deemed the act unconstitutional, however, arguing that Congress had no power to regulate the conduct of individuals. This ruling led to the withdrawal of federal troops from the south, effectively re-enslaving African Americans. The Supreme Court ruling Plessy v. Ferguson established in 1896 the doctrine of "Separate but Equal," which further oppressed African Americans. The Ku Klux Klan and the Chain Gang System thrived in the South through to the Civil Rights laws of the 1960s.

Despite these nearly insurmountable obstacles to achievement, African Americans made landmark contributions to American life in the fields of science, medicine, literature, sports, education, arts, entertainment, manufacturing, and law. Some were great inventors. There were nearly fifty thousand professional positions held by African Americans in the U.S. even by the end of the nineteenth century, including 21,000 teachers, 15,000 clergymen, 1,700 physicians, and nearly 1,000 lawyers. Distinguished and influential figures include Hiram Rhodes Revels, W.E.B. Du Bois, George Washington Carver, Booker T. Washington, Carter J. Woodson, Alain Locke, Marcus Garvey, Paul Robeson, Mathew Henson, Paul Laurence Dunbar, James Weldon Johnson, Fredrick Douglas Patterson (the automobile manufacturer), Dr. Rebecca Lee Crumpler, Charlotte Ray, Dr. James Durham, Edward Bannister (an artist), and George Franklin Grant (a dentist). Among athletes were the Kentucky Derby winner Oliver Lewis, baseball pioneer Moses Fleetwood Walker, world champion boxer George Dixon, and world champion cyclist Marshall "Major" Taylor.

African Americans were breaking new ground in professional sports and quickly dominated the fields of horse racing, cycling, and boxing. In William Rhoden's book, *Forty Million Dollar Slaves*, he identifies accomplished men who died in obscurity, despite excellence and achievement in sports, even during the worst Jim Crow times around the turn of the twentieth century. The "Jockey Syndrome," which changed rules retroactively, suppressed African American dominance in horse racing, and later spread to baseball, cycling, boxing, football, and basketball. Blacks have continued to participate in professions such as sports, the military, and entertainment, where there are perhaps the clearest measures of success. There is a level playing field—a 100-yard dash is a 100-yard dash for all runners.

The winning rider at the first Kentucky Derby in 1875 was Oliver Lewis, a black man; in that race, thirteen of the fifteen riders were black. Isaac Murphy rode and won every major stake race for the next fifteen years. His income ranged above $20,000 per year when the average worker's annual salary was about $500. He died in obscurity in 1891, at only thirty-five. Jimmy Winkfield won the 1901 and 1902 Kentucky Derby races, but was chased out of racing by the Jockey Syndrome. He was invited to eastern Europe to race and became a wealthy star. He later moved to France, bought a farm, and ran a successful stable business. He was invited back to the Kentucky Derby in 1960 to be honored for his earlier wins, but he was refused entrance to the hotel.

There were many African Americans who, while living under great oppression during this period, led lives of pride and dignity. They worked hard, raised families, and remained optimistic about their future. In this chapter, "Hearts and Souls," we honor them with the eloquent images of their faces, though their names are lost to history.

Tintypes, ca. 1855–1900
Makers unknown
Tintype
2 ½ x 3 ½ in. – 3 ½ x 5 ½ in.

The first permanent photograph was produced in 1826 by a French inventor, Joseph Niépce. Tintypes were first described in 1853, a derivative form in which a wet photographic emulsion on a thin sheet of blackened iron (not tin, as the name would imply) was exposed to light through a lens and camera and then processed in chemicals to make the image permanent. Because of the speed of the process, which took only a few minutes, the low cost, and the short exposure times, tintypes were the most popular form of portrait photography after 1850, until the invention of negative film displaced it around 1890. Tintypes were very durable and many, like the ones shown on these pages, have

survived to present day.

These tintypes have come to us without any documentation, and the names of the people have long been lost to history, but these proud and dynamic portraits suggest scenarios of achievement and accomplishment. As a group they provide a collective snapshot of the accomplishments of African Americans after the end of the Civil War, until their newfound freedoms were extinguished by repressive legislation and Supreme Court decisions toward the end of the nineteenth century.

Tintypes, ca. 1855–1900
Makers unknown
Tintype
2 ½ x 3 ½ in.

Young girl, ca. 1855
Maker unknown
Ambrotype
3 ¾ x 3 ¼ x ¾ in.

Well-to-do black couple, ca. 1860
Maker unknown
Hand-colored tintype
3 ¾ x 3 ¼ x ¾ in.

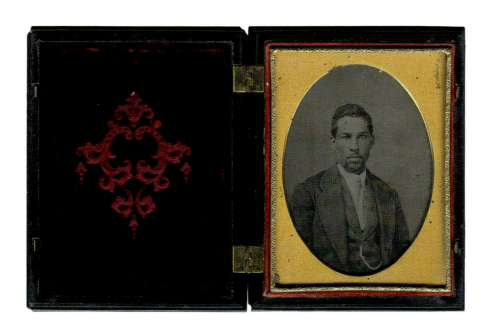

Portrait of young black gentleman, ca. 1860
Maker unknown
Ambrotype
4 x 5 x 1 in.

Picking Cotton, San Benito, Texas

"Day Nursery"

Unknown Workers

Unknown Workers

Convicts Grading Railroad, Laurinburg, N.C.

Postcards, ca. early 20th century
Makers unknown
Photographic post cards
3 ½ x 5 ½ in.

These photographic postcards are literally snapshots of the harsh realities of life for African Americans in the south in the early 20th century. After the failure of the post Civil War "era of reconstruction" in the late 19th century, life for African Americans in the south returned to near slave-like conditions.

Segregation was legalized. The Ku Klux Klan used threats and violence to control much of the politics. Share cropping, a system where tenant farmers paid rent by giving a portion of their harvest to the land owner, became the primary livelihood for African Americans. African American men were convicted and

sentenced to jail for all kinds of minor charges where they were then hired out for labor on "chain gangs." Douglas Blackmon descibes this period of "neo slavery" in his Pulitzer Prize winning book *Slavery by Another Name*.

The Boss, 2006
Bisa Butler
Quilted cotton, appliqué
34 x 21 in.

Forging Freedom

There may be times when we are powerless to prevent injustice, but there must never be a time when we fail to protest.

— Elie Wiesel

Bernard and Shirley Kinsey came of age during the fight for civil rights, one of the most powerful movements in modern history. Both were actively engaged in that cause. Shirley was arrested and jailed for participating in a demonstration at Florida A&M University, and she met Bernard soon after her release. The right to citizenship, which inspired the struggles of the civil rights movement, informs their collecting efforts.

Frederick Douglass, Benjamin Banneker, and Carrie Kinsey, whether famous or virtually unknown, all contributed to the cause of social justice and fought for the rights and agency of those who could not speak for themselves. The Kinseys continue to assemble artifacts that tell the story of forging freedom, beginning with Reconstruction.

Reconstruction saw the end of slavery, the temporary equalization of black and white men, and the establishment of provisions for reparations to freed slaves. During this time, many African Americans were elected to public office, several serving in the United States Congress, including Hiram Rhoades Revels, the first African American senator, representing Mississippi in the 41st and 42nd Congress. Bernard Kinsey has collected the images and signatures of these men, who are often forgotten or even parodied in modern references to this era.

African Americans faced formidable challenges at this time, including the dissolution of the principles of Reconstruction and the emergence of "Black Codes," which had their roots in the Civil War–era slave codes. In the 1870s, large groups of lawless whites terrorized blacks in the South. Toward the end of the decade, white militia groups carried out open violence against blacks. Groups such as the White League, the Ku Klux Klan, and the Red Shirts formed to provide paramilitary support for the Southern Democratic Party. These groups helped secure the near total disenfranchisement of black voters through poll taxes, literacy tests, and grandfather clauses, as well as extreme acts of violence.

There are over two hundred documented incidents of white-on-black persecution during this era. Some blacks were literally burned out of their homes. Following these incidents, the refugees sought safe haven in other places and recounted the hateful crimes committed against them in powerful oratory. One of the best documented incidents occurred in Rosewood, Florida, in 1923. Victims of that atrocity fled to nearby Fort White and Gainesville. Their oral history was among Bernard Kinsey's earliest childhood memories, as recounted by his father, U. B. Kinsey, who remembered their arrival. His passing down of this story profoundly influenced Bernard's commitment to the reconstruction of the past through tactile artifacts.

In the early 20th century, whites perpetuated discriminatory practices through the passage of Jim Crow laws, which imposed public segregation, essentially restoring the Black Codes. Black men and women lived with a daily bombardment of racial hatred and discrimination, yet contested their return to second-class citizenship. Every day throughout the South, individuals resisted violence and oppression.

The Kinseys honor the legacy of these 20th-century citizens, who paved the road to freedom. Along the way, some of these anonymous voices became louder than the rest, more widely recognized and more respected. The image of Paul Robeson, for example, looms large in this presentation of legacy builders, together with Malcolm X and Martin Luther King, Jr., Robeson—actor, athlete, singer, writer, Russian scholar, and resister—is one of the best-known African Americans in the world. These very well known individuals worked for something beyond their own achievements. The collection includes artists, writers, orators, and soldiers who worked for the benefit of the African American community at large, establishing the path down which the Kinseys and many others would follow.

For the Kinseys, the power of Bisa Butler's image lies in its representation of the four million African Americans who toiled on 75,000 cotton plantations, generating billions of dollars from their free labor.

The First Vote, n.d.

Gayle Hubbard

Watercolor painted on facsimile of
Harper's Weekly, November 16, 1867

20 x 16 in.

Contemporary artist Gayle Hubbard has enhanced this *Harper's Weekly* cover illustration, "The First Vote," with watercolor paint. The power of the image was recognized and promoted by the publication's editors, who wrote in 1867:

"The good sense and discretion, and above all the modesty, which the freedmen have displayed in the exercise, for the first time, of the great privilege which has been bestowed upon them, and the vast power which accompanies the privilege, have been most noticeable. Admiration of their commendable conduct has suggested the admirable engraving which we give on the first page of this issue. The freedmen are represented marching to the ballot-box to deposit their first vote, not with expressions of exultation or of defiance of their old masters and present opponents depicted on their countenances, but looking serious and solemn and determined. The picture is one which should interest every colored loyalist in the country."

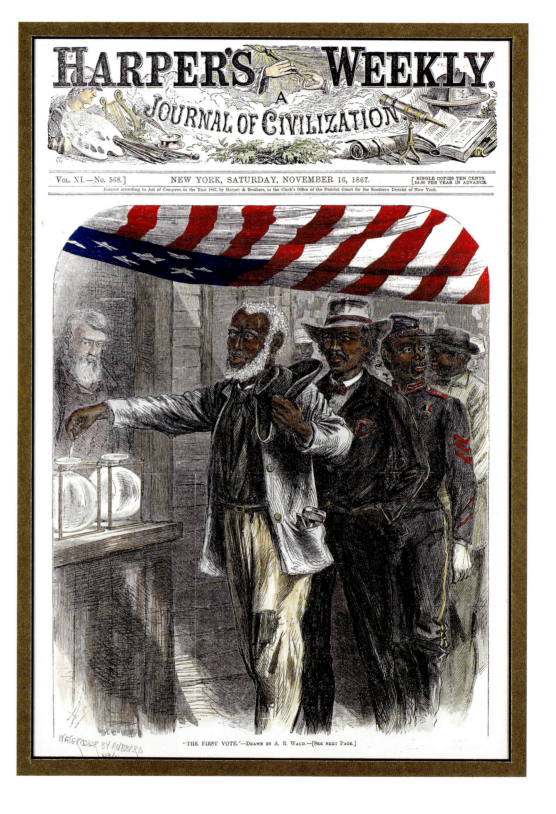

The First Colored Senator and Representatives in the 41st and 42nd US Congress, 1872
Currier and Ives
Lithograph
24 x 18 in.

Left to right: Senator Hiram Revels of Mississippi, Representatives Benjamin Turner of Alabama, Robert DeLarge of South Carolina, Josiah Walls of Florida, Jefferson Long of Georgia, and Joseph Rainey and Robert Brown Elliot of South Carolina.

Of the 22 African American men who served in the United States Congress between 1870 and 1901, 13 of them had been born into slavery. Hiram Rhoades Revels, Josiah Walls, and Robert Brown Elliot were born to free parents. Regardless of their backgrounds and the discrimination they faced in securing their seats, these men championed the rights of all Americans, proving that African Americans could succeed in the framework of a democratically elected legislature.

Josiah Walls, Congressman representing Florida

Photograph
11 x 13 in.

Josiah Walls was conscripted into the Confederate Army and was freed by Union soldiers in 1862. He joined the Union Army and was stationed in Florida, where he married and chose to reside after his discharge. He became involved in Florida politics and decided to enter the political arena in earnest in 1868. He survived an assassination attempt to become the first African American to represent Florida in Congress, where he served from 1871 to 1876. A Republican, he was the only black Congressman from Florida until 1993, when FAMU graduates Alcee Hastings, Corrine Brown, and Carrie Meek were elected to office. (Hastings and Brown still hold seats in the House of Representatives.) Walls, repeatedly challenged for his seat, was eventually defeated, but during his tenure, he represented the needs of his state effectively and championed public education. Later in life, Walls worked at Florida Normal College, now known as Florida A&M University, and died in obscurity on May 15, 1905.

BRADY, PHOTO., NEW YORK.

Hiram Rhoades Revels, ca. 1870
Mathew Brady
Cabinet card photograph
13 ¼ x 10 ¾ in.

Hiram Rhoades Revels, who was of mixed African and American Indian descent, represented the state of Mississippi as the first black senator elected during Reconstruction. He founded Alcorn State College, still in existence today as Alcorn State University.

NORTH CAROLINA LAW

Providing for the Separate Accommodation of White & Colored Passengers Upon Motor Busses, and for Other Purposes.

General Statutes No. 60-135. Separate accommodations for different races; failure to provide misdemeanor.—All street, interurban and suburban railway companies, engaged as common carriers in the transportation of passengers for hire in the state of North Carolina, shall provide and set apart so much of the front portion of each car operated by them as shall be necessary, for occupation by the white passengers therein, and shall likewise provide and set apart so much of the rear part of such car as shall be necessary, for occupation by the colored passengers therein, and shall require as far as practicable the white and colored passengers to occupy the respective parts of such car so set apart for each of them. The provisions of this section shall not apply to nurses or attendants of children or of the sick or infirm of a different race, while in attendance upon such children or such sick or infirm persons. Any officer, agent or other employee of any street railway company who shall willfully violate the provisions of this section shall be guilty of a misdemeanor, and upon conviction shall be fined or imprisoned in the discretion of the court.

General Statutes No. 60-136. Passengers to take certain seats; violation of requirement misdemeanor.—Any white person entering a street car or other passenger vehicle or motor bus for the purpose of becoming a passenger therein shall, in order to carry out the purposes of Sec. No. 60-135, occupy the first vacant seat or unoccupied space nearest the front thereof, and any colored person entering a street car or other passenger vehicle or motor bus for a like purpose shall occupy the first vacant seat or unoccupied space nearest the rear end thereof, provided, however, that no contiguous seat on the same bench shall be occupied by white and colored passengers at the same time, unless and until all the other seats in the car have been occupied. Upon request of the person in charge of the street car or other passenger vehicle or motor bus, and when necessary in order to carry out the purpose of providing separate seats for white and colored passengers, it shall be the duty of any white person to move to any unoccupied seat toward or in the front of the car, vehicle or bus, and the duty of any colored person to move to any unoccupied seat toward or in the rear thereof, and the failure of any such person to so move shall constitute prima facie evidence of an intent to violate this section. Any person violating the provisions of this section shall be guilty of a misdemeanor and, upon conviction, shall be fined not more than fifty dollars or imprisoned not exceeding thirty days. Any such person may also be ejected from the car, vehicle or bus by the person charged with the operation thereof. Each person now or hereafter charged with the operation of any such street car, passenger vehicle or motor bus is hereby invested with police powers and authority to carry out the provisions of this section.

General Statutes No. 60-137. No liability for mistake in assigning passengers to wrong seat.—No street, suburban or interurban railway company, its agents, servants or employees, shall be liable to any person on account of any mistake in the designation of any passenger to a seat or part of a car set apart for passengers of the other race.

General Statutes No. 60-138. Misconduct on car; riding on front platform misdemeanor.—It shall be unlawful for any passenger to expectorate upon the floor or any other part of any street car, or to use, while thereon, any loud, profane or indecent language, or to make any insulting or disparaging remark to or about any other passenger or person thereon within his or her hearing. It shall likewise be unlawful for any passenger to stand willfully upon the front platform, fender, bumper, running-board or steps of such car while the same is in motion, whether such passenger has or has not paid the usual fare for riding on such car. Any person willfully violating any of the provisions of this section shall be guilty of a misdemeanor, and upon conviction shall be fined not more than fifty dollars or imprisoned not exceeding thirty days. He may also be ejected from the car by the conductor and other agent or agents charged with the operation of such car, who are hereby invested with police powers to carry out the provisions of this section.

General Statutes No. 60-139. Sections 60-135 to 60-138 extended to motor busses used as common carriers.—The provisions of Sections 60-135 to 60-138 are hereby extended to motor busses operated in the urban, interurban or suburban transportation of passengers for hire, and to the operator or operators thereof, and the agents, servants, and employees of such operators.

PASSENGERS ARE WARNED NOT TO RIDE ON THE PLATFORM

**North Carolina Law Providing for Separate
Accommodation for White & Colored Passengers
Upon Motor Busses, and for Other Purposes, 1907**

Printed document
6 ¼ x 13 ¼ in.

The 1896 United States Supreme Court decision *Plessy v. Ferguson* established that "separate" facilities for blacks and whites were constitutional as long as they were "equal." The "separate but equal" doctrine was extended through state legislation to cover many areas of public life, such as restaurants, theaters, restrooms, and public schools.

The state laws were posted in public spaces to ensure that they were obeyed. Although separate accommodations for blacks were rarely equal to those of whites, the local, state, and federal governments upheld the Supreme Court ruling as a strategy for racial dominance and the continued subjugation of blacks.

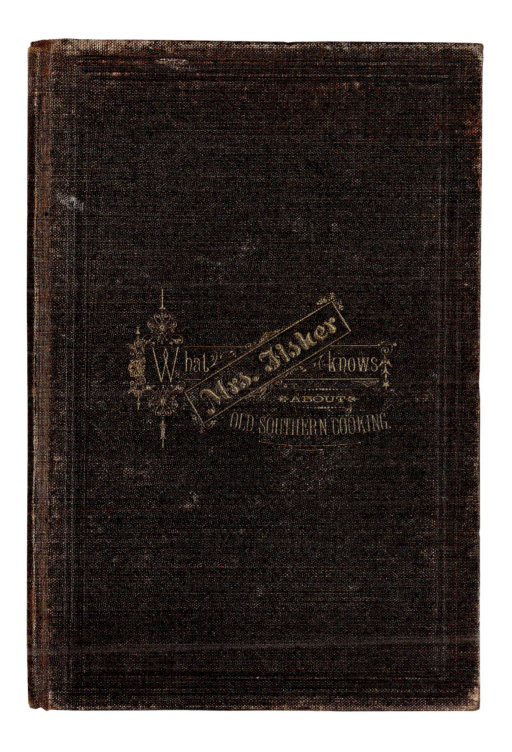

What Mrs. Fisher Knows About Old Southern Cooking, Soups, Pickles, Preserves, etc., 1881
Abby Fisher
Original publisher's brown pebbled-cloth book, stamped in gilt
7 ¾ x 5 ½ x ¾ in.

Abby Fisher, born a slave, could not read or write. In the 1880 census, Mrs. Fisher is listed by race—mulatto—and profession—cook. Her husband, also a mulatto, Alexander Fisher, born in Mobile, Alabama, is listed as well. The couple arrived in San Francisco around 1870, with their eleven children, and Mrs. Fisher began to gain a reputation as a cook and as a pickle and preserve maker. She was awarded a diploma at the Sacramento State Fair in 1879. At the San Francisco Mechanics Institute Fair of 1889, she won medals for best pickles and sauces and for best assortment of jellies and preserves.

This cookbook is the first by an African American. Nine prominent white San Franciscans, three men and six women, transcribed Fisher's recipes and published the cookbook through the prolific Women's Co-operative Printing Union.

Letter to President Roosevelt, 1903
Carrie Kinsey
Digital scan
8 x 10 in

This letter from Carrie Kinsey, Bernard Kinsey's second cousin, demonstrates the Kinsey family traits of persistence and intelligence, and the passion for justice and mobility in the face of the brutal culture that existed particularly in the South after the Civil War and Reconstruction. Although she is largely illiterate, she understands that the President of the United States is her only redress. She writes:

Mr. President I have a brother about 14 years old a colord man came hear a hird him from me and sad that he would take good care of him an pay me five dollars a month for him an I heard of him no more he went an sold him to Macree an tha tha [they] has bin working him in prison for 12 month and I has tried to get thim to sind him to me an tha wont let/him go he has no mother and has no father they are both dead an I am his only friend an tha wont let me have him he hase not don nothing for thim to have him in chanes so I rite to yoo for yoo to help me get my poor brother – his name is James Robinson and the man that carried him of his name Darr Cal he sold him to McCra at Valdosta, Ga please let me hear from yoo at once.

Carrie Kinsey

Carrie Kinsey's letter provided the impetus for Douglas Blackmon's 2008 book, *Slavery by Another Name,* which won a Pulitzer Prize in 2009. In April of 2009, Bernard and Shirley traveled with Blackmon to the National Archives in Washington, D.C., to retrieve the letter. It is one of the most personal and important acquisitions in their collection.

Receipt of letter, 1903
Department of Justice
Digital scan
10 x 2 ½ in.

From: Blackmon, Doug
To: bernardkinsey
Sent: Friday, August 08, 2008 11:59 AM
Subject: Carrie Kinsey letter

Bernard,
Attached is the PDF of the envelope and Carrie Kinsey letter on file at the National Archives. Before you read on, I want to tell you that I discovered this letter about six years ago, and I have carried it in my mind and my heart since that day. There a handful of stories and specific pieces of evidence discovered in my research that I have been unable to fully come to terms with. This is the most potent of those. It had been a couple of years since I last held it in my hand until I dug it back out for you this week. When I first reread the entire letter, I felt that same initial rush of grief and horror that struck me the first time I ever saw it.

I am thrilled to be able to share it with you, because of your deep desire and need to know this whole story. At the same time, I confess that it also worries me at some level. The emotion and tragedy and abandonment and travesty of our national ideals that are woven through this brief letter are heartbreaking to me. It fills me with shame, as a white person and as an American.

I wanted to say that to you before you go any further.
Doug

The two attached images are prints made from microfilm of the collection: "Peonage Files of the U.S. Department of Justice, 1901-1945." More than 30,000 pages are contained in the collection, but I'm certain we can locate the original in Washington D.C.

Carrie's letter is almost impossible to read on the copy and in the PDF, but here is my transcription of the full letter. Also, note that the numbers stamped on the two pages (000171 and 000172) and the "A" with a circle around it on one page don't mean anything as far as locating the original. Those are part of my filing system, and do not appear on the original document.

Here is the text:

> Bainbridge, GA July 26, 1903
> Mr pressident I
> have a brother about 14 years old a
> colord man came hear a hird him from
> me and sad that he would take good
> care of him an pay me five dollars a
> month for him an I heard of him no more
> he went an sold him to Macree an tha
> tha [they] has bin working him in prison for
> 12 month and I has tried to get thim to
> sind him to me an tha wont let/him go he
> has no mother and has no farther
> they are both dead an I am his only
> friend an tha wont let me have him he
> hase not don nothing for thim to have
> him in chanes so I rite to yoo for yoo
> to help me get my poor brother--his
> name is James Robinson and the
> man that carried him of his name
> Darr Cal he sold him to McCra at
> Valdosta, Ga please let me hear from
> yoo at once
> Carrie Kinsey

Douglas A. Blackmon

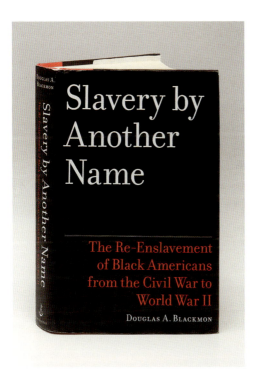

***Slavery by Another Name:
The Re-Enslavement of Black Americans
from the Civil War to World War II**, 2008*
Douglas A. Blackmon
Book
9 x 6 ½ x 1 ½ in.

Letter to Bernard Kinsey, 2008
Douglas A. Blackmon
Photomechanical reproduction
8 ½ x 11 in

Explorer Matthew Henson, 1910

Carte de visite, 7 x 5
letter, 6 ½ x 5, envelope, 6 x 3 ¼ in.

Matthew A. Henson was an explorer who became one of the first men to reach the North Pole. Robert E. Peary hired Henson on many expeditions, including the historic venture to the North Pole in 1909. Henson's account of the expedition, *A Negro Explorer at the North Pole*, was published in 1912. In 1913, President William Howard Taft appointed him a clerk in the U.S. Customs House in New York City. Henson was awarded the Congressional Medal for the Peary Expedition in 1944.

Dr. S. Allen Counter, a high school classmate and close friend of Bernard Kinsey's, worked to have Matthew Henson reburied with full honors in Arlington Cemetery .

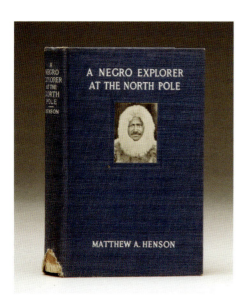

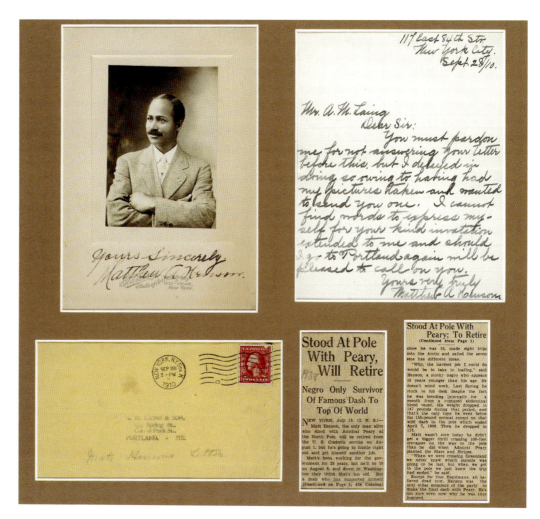

A Negro Explorer at the North Pole, 1912

Matthew Henson
Book
8 ½ x 6 x 1 in.

Commemorative coins and stamps, 1948, 1956

Booker T. Washington
Picture, 4 ¾ x 4 in
Coin, 1 ¼ diam.
Envelope, 6 ¼ x 3 ½ in.

George Washington Carver
Picture, 5 ¼ x 3 ¾ in
Coin, 1 ¼ diam.
Envelope, 6 ¼ x 3 ½ in.

Booker T. Washington was a renowned American educator, author, and orator. Born a slave, he was emancipated in 1865 and went on to become the first president of the Tuskegee Normal and Industrial Institute (now Tuskegee University). Washington was considered to be one of the most influential leaders of the African American community in the 1890s and early 1900s.

George Washington Carver was an American agricultural chemist and agronomist. Carver is known for revolutionizing agriculture in the South by conducting groundbreaking research on alternative crops to replace cotton. His experimentation with peanuts, sweet potatoes, and soybeans enabled poor farmers to cultivate crops that could provide food for their families. In 1896, Carver became the director of agricultural research for the Tuskegee Normal and Industrial Institute, where he worked with Booker T. Washington. Carver's many accomplishments include his election to Britain's Society for the Encouragement of Arts, Manufactures, and Commerce in 1916 and the award of the Spingarn Medal in 1923 .

World War I Postcards, ca.1919
Makers unknown
Photographic post cards
3 ½ x 5 ½ in.

Featured in the center is a portrait postcard of Lieutenant Benedict Mosley wearing the French Croix de Guerre Medal for the Battle of Argonne, which he and his fellow "Harlem Hellfighters" of the 9th Calvary 369th Infantry Regiment were awarded by the French Military.

The remaining four portrait postcards are unidentified members of the more than 350,000 African American soldiers and sailors who served in highly segregated units, mostly as support troops, during World War I. Lower right is a rare image of an African American woman Navy Corporal.

CITATION FOR CROIX DE GUERRE

AWARDED
369ᵉ RÉGIMENT d'INFANTERIE U. S.

(FORMERLY 15ᵗʰ N. Y. INFANTRY)

FOR ITS OPERATIONS AS A COMBAT UNIT OF A FRENCH

DIVISION IN THE GREAT OFFENSIVE IN

CHAMPAGNE, SEPT. AND OCT. 1918,

BY THE FRENCH COMMANDING GENERAL

Sous le Commandement du Colonel HAYWARD qui, bien que blessé, a tenu à conduire son régiment au combat, du Lieutenant Colonel PICKERING, admirable de sang-froid et de courage, du Commandant COBB (tué), du Commandant SPENCER (grièvement blessé), du Commandant LITTLE véritable entraineur d'hommes, le 369ᵉ R. I. U. S. qui lors des attaques de Septembre 1918, voyait le feu pour la première fois, s'est emparé de puissantes organisations ennemies, énergiquement défendues et a enlevé de haute lutte le village de S . . . ., a fait des prisonniers, ramené 6 canons et un grand nombre de mitrailleuses.

TRANSLATION

Under command of Colonel HAYWARD, who, though injured, insisted on leading his regiment in the battle, of Lieutenant Colonel PICKERING, admirably cool and brave, of Major COBB, (killed), of Major SPENCER (grievously wounded), of Major LITTLE, a true leader of men, the 369ᵗʰ R. I. U. S. engaging in an offensive for the first time in the drive of September, 1918 stormed powerful enemy positions energetically defended, took, after heavy fighting, the town of S . . . ., captured prisoners and brought back six cannons and a great number of machine guns.

***Citation for Croix de Guerre,** 1918*
Government of France
Printed document
8 ½ x 11 in.

The French Government awarded the 369th Infantry Regiment, the Harlem Hellfighters, its Croix de Guerre (Cross of War) for specific acts of bravery in capturing the village of Séchault from German forces during the regiment's service with French troops in World War I.

The 369th Infantry took part in many campaigns in Europe and was the first Allied force to reach the Rhine River in Germany. In addition, the 369th band introduced jazz to much of Europe, creating a musical phenomenon in both the cities and the countryside.

By the end of the war, many soldiers in the division were awarded French Medals of Honor; however, they would return to the United States to face increasing racial hostility and blatant acts of discrimination. They returned home changed men, by both the war and the cultural knowledge they gained. This knowledge would help create opportunities in both America and Europe for a new generation of black American artists and scholars, changing the global artistic and intellectual landscape forever.

Marcus Garvey, ca. 1920

Provisional President of Africa, Founder and President of the Universal Negro Improvement Association
Poster
19 ½ x 15 ½ in.

Marcus Mosiah Garvey was born in Jamaica on August 17, 1887, and at 14 became an apprentice in the printing trade. He moved to Kingston and helped form the Printer's Union, the first trade union in Jamaica. In 1910, Garvey was transformed from an individual concerned about people with little opportunity to an African nationalist determined to lift an entire race from bondage.

Garvey's movement, headquartered in New York, was the greatest international movement of African peoples in modern times. From 1922 to 1924, the movement claimed to have over eight million followers. Garvey emphasized the belief in one God, the God of Africa, who should be seen through black eyes. He preached to black people, urging them to know their African history and their rich cultural heritage. He was the first voice to clearly demand black power: "A race without authority and power is a race without respect." He was imprisoned for securities fraud and spent nearly three years in jail. He was deported back to Jamaica and died in London in 1940.

First Provisional President of Africa

FOUNDER *and* PRESIDENT-GENERAL OF
THE
UNIVERSAL NEGRO IMPROVEMENT
ASSOCIATION

The Birth of a Race Photoplay Corporation
Certificate of 10 shares of stock in the Corporation, 1918
Standard engraved certificate
8 x 11 in.

This is a stock certificate from one of the earliest black film companies, formed to rebut D. W. Griffith's *Birth of a Nation*. Emmett J. Scott, best known for *Scott's Official History of the American Negro in the World War*, formed "The Birth of a Race Photoplay Corporation" in 1917 with a capital stock of a million dollars. The company undertook one of the largest stock offerings ever, signing up approximately 7,000 shareholders for a total of $140,000.

A Documented History of the Incident Which Occurred at Rosewood, Florida, in January 1923, 1993

Jones, Rivers, Colburn, Dye, and Rogers
Photomechanical reproduction
8 ½ x 11 in.

In January 1923, black townspeople of Rosewood acted to defend themselves after one of them was lynched over the accusation that a white woman was attacked, and possibly raped, by a black man. When several hundred whites burned the community of Rosewood to the ground, the black residents fled, and they never returned.

This report provided the documentation necessary for the survivors and their descendants to be compensated for damages by the state of Florida. This is the only time reparations have been paid to black Americans for the atrocities committed against them. Florida has since declared Rosewood a Florida Heritage Landmark.

This document was a gift from
Dr Larry E. Rivers.

**A DOCUMENTED HISTORY OF THE INCIDENT
WHICH OCCURRED
AT
ROSEWOOD, FLORIDA,
IN
JANUARY 1923**

SUBMITTED TO THE
FLORIDA BOARD OF REGENTS
DECEMBER 22, 1993

THE INVESTIGATIVE TEAM:

Principal Investigator:
Associate Professor Maxine D. Jones
The Florida State University

Co-Project Director:
Professor Larry E. Rivers
Florida Agricultural and Mechanical University

Professor David R. Colburn
The University of Florida

R. Tom Dye
The Florida State University

Professor William W. Rogers
The Florida State University

Rosewood: Chronology of Events

08/05/20

Four black men in McClenny are removed from the local jail and lynched for the alleged rape of a white woman.

11/02/20

Two whites and at least five blacks are killed in Ocoee in a dispute over voting rights. The black community of Ocoee is destroyed, twenty-five homes, two churches, and a Masonic Lodge.

2/12/21

A black man in Wauchula is lynched for an alleged attack on a white woman.

12/09/22

A black man in Perry is burned at the stake, accused of the murder of a white school teacher. A black church, school, Masonic Lodge, and meeting hall are burned.

12/31/22

On New Year's Eve a large Ku Klux Klan parade is held in Gainesville.

01/01/23

Early morning: Fannie Taylor reports an attack by an unidentified black man.

Monday afternoon: Aaron Carrier is apprehended by a posse and is taken out of the area by Sheriff Walker.

Late afternoon: A posse of white vigilantes apprehends and kills a black man named Sam Carter.

01/02/23

Armed whites begin gathering in Sumner.

01/04/23

Late evening: White vigilantes attack the Carrier house. Two white men are killed, and several others wounded. A black woman, Sarah Carrier, is killed, and others inside the Carrier house are either killed or wounded. Rosewood's black residents flee into the swamps.

One black church is burned, in addition to several unprotected homes.

Lexie Gordon is murdered.

01/05/23

Approximately 200 to 300 whites from surrounding areas begin to converge on Rosewood.

Mingo Williams is murdered.

Governor Cary Hardee is notified, and Sheriff Walker reports that he fears "no further disorder."

The sheriff of Alachua County arrives in Rosewood to assist Sheriff Walker.

James Carrier is murdered.

01/06/23

A train of evacuated refugees travels to Gainesville.

01/07/23

A mob of 100 to 150 whites returns to Rosewood and burns the remaining structures.

01/17/23

A black man in Newberry is convicted of stealing cattle. He is removed from his cell and lynched by local whites.

02/11/23

A grand jury convenes in Bronson to investigate the Rosewood riot.

02/15/23

The grand jury finds "insufficient evidence" to prosecute.

Panoramic photograph of the 39th Annual Conference of the NAACP, 1938
Maker unknown
Silver print
8 x 29 ½ in.

Seated in the center of this group photograph is Walter White, then National Secretary of the NAACP. To the right are Assistant National Secretary Roy Wilkins, and Thurgood Marshall, then NAACP special counsel. He was appointed to this position in 1938. Individuals seated include NAACP staff: Juanita Jackson, Dorothy Lampkin, Charles Hamilton Houston, James McClendon, E. F. Morrow, and William Pickens.

Founded on February 12, 1909, the centennial of Abraham Lincoln's birth, the NAACP is the nation's oldest, largest, and most widely recognized grassroots civil rights organization. Its more than half-million members and supporters throughout the United States and the world are the premier advocates for civil rights in their communities, campaigning for equal opportunity and conducting voter mobilization. The NAACP was formed partly in response to the horrific practice of lynching and the 1908 race riot in Springfield, the capital of Illinois and the resting place of Abraham Lincoln. Appalled at the violence that was committed against blacks, a group of white liberals that included Mary White Ovington and Oswald Garrison Villard (both descendants of abolitionists), William English Walling, and Dr. Henry Moscowitz issued a call for a meeting to discuss racial justice. Some sixty people, seven of whom were African American (including W. E. B. Du Bois, Ida B. Wells-Barnett, and Mary Church Terrell), signed the call.

The NAACP established its national office in New York City in 1910 and named a board of directors as well as a president, Moorfield Storey, who was a white constitutional lawyer and former president of the American Bar Association. Du Bois, the only African

29TH ANNUAL CONFERENCE N.A.A.C.P.
COLUMBUS, OHIO
June 28 – July 3, 1938

American among the organization's executives, was made director of publications and research and in 1910 established the official journal of the NAACP, *The Crisis*. With a strong emphasis on local organizing, by 1913 the NAACP had established branch offices in such cities as Boston, Baltimore, Kansas City, Washington, D.C., Detroit, and St. Louis. Joel Spingarn, a professor of literature who was one of the NAACP founders, formulated much of the strategy that led to the growth of the organization. He was elected board chairman of the NAACP in 1915 and served as president from 1929 to 1939. In 1938, the association

continued its fight to end segregation at the Tennessee Valley Authority. Charles Houston and Thurgood Marshall conducted a third NAACP investigation of working conditions there and submitted a report to a joint committee of Congress that was appointed to study repeated discrimination. During that same year, Thurgood Marshall was appointed NAACP special counsel after the current office holder, Charles H. Houston, returned to private practice. It was Houston who represented Lloyd Gaines before the Supreme Court in a landmark case later that year, where the Supreme Court ruled that the

University of Missouri Law School could not exclude Gaines because of his color. It also ruled that each state must provide equal educational facilities for black students, and that states could not fulfill this requirement by providing scholarships to black students to attend college elsewhere.

American Beach Negro Ocean Playground, ca. 1930

Maker unknown

Steel plaque

11 ¼ x 4 ½ in.

This plaque is an important artifact for Shirley Kinsey, as this was one of the only beaches where her family was allowed to visit and vacation. It also demonstrates the spirit common in the African American communities facing segregation up and down the Atlantic seaboard. Whites designated this beach as a segregated space, keeping their own beaches "whites only," but blacks protected, built on, and fortified their beach communities, making them into thriving and celebratory spaces.

American Beach, founded in 1935 by Florida's first black millionaire, Abraham Lincoln Lewis, was designated a historic site by the National Register of Historic Places in January 2002.

Separate Drinking Fountain, Montgomery, Alabama, 1931

Painted bronze plaque

10 ¾ x 4 ½ in

A gift from friends Erika and Eusebius Williams.

Paul Robeson in the *Song of Freedom*, 1936
Song of Freedom, Inc.
Offset lithograph
42 ½ x 29 in.

Paul Robeson was an accomplished scholar, actor, singer, and international advocate for human rights. He attended Rutgers University and Columbia Law School. He acted on the stage, including his famous Broadway portrayal of Othello, and in several films, including Oscar Micheaux's *Body and Soul*. His rendition of *Ol' Man River* became a battle cry for workmen's rights all over the world.

Robeson was fluent in Russian and spent much time in Russia, where his name is widely recognized and praised. He was targeted by the House Un-American Activities under Joseph McCarthy, and his passport was revoked in 1950. When it was reinstated in 1958, Robeson continued his travels, lecturing and singing all over the world for peace and justice. He vowed, "I shall take my voice wherever there are those who want to hear the melody of freedom or the words that might inspire hope and courage in the face of fear. My weapons are peaceful. For it is only by peace that peace can be attained. The song of freedom must prevail." Robeson died in 1976.

Brown et al vs. Board of Education of Topeka et al, 1954
Typed on paper
8 ½ x 11 in.

Brown v. Board of Education was the landmark case that overturned *Plessy v. Ferguson,* which in 1896 upheld the "separate but equal" principle. The decision in Brown was bolstered by several national precedents that chipped away at the constitutionality of *Plessy*. Bernard Kinsey's father, U.B. Kinsey, was involved in two of those early cases. One occurred in 1941, when he was a member of the Palm Beach County Teachers Association, which successfully sued the local board of education for equal pay. The suit was argued by Thurgood Marshall who, with his colleagues, would win the Supreme Court's unanimous approval for the desegregation of public school in *Brown*.

May 17, 1954

Brown et al vs. Board of Education of Topeka et al

"We come then to the question presented: Does segregation of children in public schools solely on the basis of race, even though the physical facilities and other 'tangible' factors may be equal, deprive the children of the minority group of equal educational opportunities? We believe that it does."

"We conclude that in the field of public education the doctrine of 'separate but equal' has no place. Separate educational facilities are inherently unequal."

Malik Shabazz

153 Lenox Avenue   New York 26, N. Y.

AC 2-6522-3

December 3, 1963

Mr. Alex Haley
P. O. Box 110
Rome, N. Y.

Dear Mr. Haley:

This is just a brief note to let you know that I will
probably be available almost any day between now and
the end of the year. I have cancelled all public
appearances and speaking engagements for the rest of
the year and even perhaps into January. So, within
that period it should be possible to finish this book.
With the fast pace of newly developing incidents today,
it is easy for something that is done or said tomorrow
to be outdated even by sunset on the same day.

Hoping to hear from you soon.

Sincerely,

Malcolm X.

MX:mex

Letter to Alex Haley, 1963
Malcolm X
Typed on paper
8.5 x 11 in.

Bernard Kinsey is a student of history. The documents he collects are a conduit to an African American past to which he links both his mobility and his legacy. While some artifacts, such as this one, are written by iconic figures, many in the Kinsey Collection document the extraordinary courage of the common man—each contributing to the tapestry of black history that the Kinseys are assembling, in order to educate and inspire those who encounter it.

Letter from Rev. Dr. Martin Luther King, Jr. to his Literary Agent, 1957
Typed on paper
8 ½ x 11 in.

King's letterhead identifies him as Pastor of the Dexter Avenue Baptist Church and President of the Montgomery Improvement Association. Written to his literary agent, Mary Rodell, the letter refers to the contract for his first book, *Strive Toward Freedom*.

Martin Luther King, Jr.
309 South Jackson Street
Montgomery, Alabama

Minister
Dexter Avenue Baptist Church
454 Dexter Avenue

November 13, 1957

President
Montgomery Improvement
Association Inc.
530 South Union Street

Mrs. Marie Rodell
Literary Agent
15 East 48th Street
New York 17, New York

Dear Mrs. Rodell:

Enclosed is the Harper contract with my signature. I have read the contract very scrutinizingly. I have also read each of the suggestions that Pauli Murray made. I would like to ask you to urge Harpers to make the changes that Pauli Murray suggested under her points 1, 2, 3, 5, and 6. Points 4, 7, 8, 9, and 11 need not be pressed.

I will be keeping in touch with you as my writing progresses. I am still working hard to have the first draft completed by the first of December. You will be receiving some chapters from me in a few days.

Very sincerely yours,

M. L. King, Jr.

MLK:mlb

Enclosure

Woolworth Boycott Broadside by CORE, ca. 1960
Ink on paper
8 ¼ x 10 ¾ in.

The first sit-ins by the Congress of Racial Equality in Chicago in 1943 were intended to change the attitudes of business owners—as did this one of 1960, a national boycott of Woolworth's.

During the period 1955–68, acts of nonviolent protest and civil disobedience produced confrontations between activists and government authorities. Crisis situations that highlighted the inequities faced by African Americans often drew immediate attention from federal, state, and local governments, and from businesses and educational institutions. Forms of protest and/or civil disobedience included boycotts, such as the successful Montgomery Bus Boycott in Alabama (1955–1956); sit-ins such as the influential Greensboro one in North Carolina (1960); marches, such as the Selma to Montgomery marches in Alabama (1965); and a wide range of other nonviolent activities.

Many of those who were active in the civil rights movement, with organizations such as NAACP, SNCC, CORE, and SCLC, prefer the term "Southern Freedom Movement" because the struggle was about far more than just civil rights under the law; it was also about fundamental issues of freedom, respect, dignity, and economic and social equality.

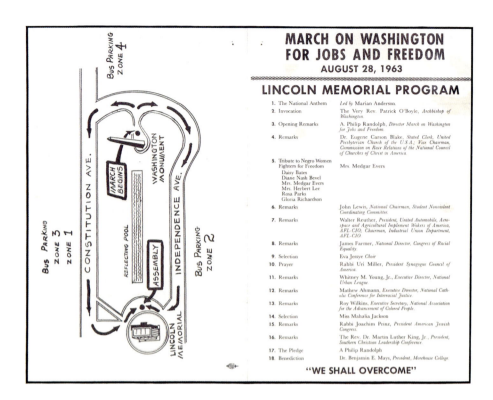

**March on Washington for Jobs and Freedom,
August 28, 1963**
Lincoln Memorial program with news photograph of
Martin Luther King, Jr.
Ink on paper and black-and-white photograph
8 ½ x 18 ¾ in.

This is the original program from the March on Washington for Jobs and Freedom, calling for racial equality and an end to discrimination. The speech by Dr. King, famously known as "I Have a Dream," was delivered from the steps of the Lincoln Memorial to over 200,000 rapt listeners. The speech galvanized the burgeoning civil rights movement and awakened the social conscience of the American people. It is without question one of the greatest speeches given in the history of the United States.

Here is an excerpt from the program:

"It was conceived as an outpouring of the deep feeling of millions of white and colored American citizens that the time has come for the government of the United States of America, and particularly for the Congress of that government, to grant and guarantee complete equality and citizenship of the Negro minority of our population. As such, the Washington March is a living petition— in the flesh—of

the scores of thousands of citizens of both races who will be present from all parts of our country."

Major legislative landmarks consequent on the movement are the Civil Rights Act of 1964 and the Voting Rights Act of 1965.

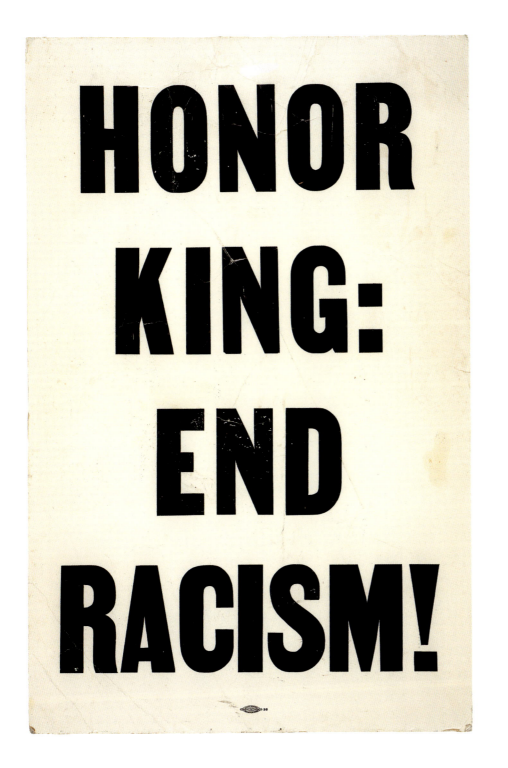

Honor King: End Racism! 1968
Ink on board
14 x 21 in.

This placard was carried during the memorial march in honor of Dr. Martin Luther King, Jr., held on April 8, 1968, in Memphis, Tennessee.

Memorial March after the Assassination of Martin Luther King, Jr., 1968
Ernest Withers
Silver print
16 x 24 in.

Reflections

Beauty is in the eyes, heart, and soul of the collector…

We think of ourselves not as owners of art but as caretakers, sharing a story, not possessions. Many of the artists' works we collect have caught my eye, captured my heart, and remain in my soul. Our journey of discovery is remarkable, as we have been blessed to make and maintain relationships along the way. Artists and friends such as Ernie Barnes, Phoebe Beasley, Artis Lane, Ed Dwight, Jonathan Green, and Tina Allen: all touched our lives in profound ways, very early on and very directly.

The themes in Ernie Barnes' figurative painting style captured both of us, with the elongated limbs of his young subjects playing in dirt yards, boys playing basketball and girls jumping rope. His images inspired us and brought back childhood memories at the same time. His *High Aspirations* shows a young man reaching high and dunking a basketball into a hoop made from a peach basket attached to a plywood backboard, mounted on a pole. It became our symbol of someone striving to do their best and attaining that goal.

In 1977, Bernard began to give a Barnes print to his top performing sales people. Instead of the usual plaque, they proudly took home to hang on their walls a work of art: Ernie Barnes' *High Aspirations*, framed and inscribed with their name and stats. Some years later we met Ernie and became friends, and he let us know that his inspiration for *Homecoming* was our alma mater's band, the Florida A&M University Marching 100. Bernard had played in this band, and we are both so very proud of their work. Needless to say, that strengthened our connection to Ernie, and he will always have a place in our hearts and in our home… We miss him.

We knew of Phoebe Beasley in the early 1980s and immediately felt drawn to her work. We attended an auction held by the Museum of African American Art, and when our son Khalil saw one of her paintings, he asked to bid. He was about eight years old at the time, and he acquired the piece: a 1973 watercolor with eight young African American boys and girls with words that spoke to him even then. That led to a lifelong friendship.

Loving Phoebe's images of grandmotherly figures was a big part of getting to know and love her as a friend. The sensitivity she shows in the themes of her work, her use of fabric, paper, ribbon, cardboard, and paint gives an insight into the spirit that lives in her creativity. In 1987, we commissioned her to do a special piece for our dear friends Joe and Julie Johnson, upon his retirement from Xerox. In Phoebe's creative style, she asked for and used fabric and other family items to personalize a unique work of art. I continue to collect her work for us as well. Her print *Holding Court* hangs in my personal space; *Piano, Bass and Drums* is in the exhibit; and my own portrait, *Shirley*, hangs at home.

Artis Lane … what a fortuitous name. We were first exposed to her work in 1985, and loved her portraits and sculptures immediately. Soon bonds were formed with her and her husband, Vince. Imagine how delighted we were to have her commissioned by the Xerox Black Employees to do a portrait of our son, Khalil, as a gift to us when Bernard retired in 1991. Little did we know that 11 years later we would be given a portrait of us as a 35th wedding anniversary gift from our FAMU best friend, Thomas L. Mitchell, with friends Terry and Thelma Harris. This highly spiritual and creative lady recently had the honor of having her bust of Sojourner Truth placed in the U.S. Capitol by our First Lady, Michelle Obama. Artis is keeping our history alive.

Ed Dwight came to us in 1986 by way of a gallery in Maui. We saw his magnificent sculpture of Charlie Parker, and upon hearing his story, that he was an astronaut in training, we wondered out loud how it was that we didn't know this man. Bernard called him in Denver, invited him to the Urban League Dinner in Los Angeles, and the rest is living history. His sculptures of strong African women spoke so directly to me and his jazz pieces and Revolutionary soldiers spoke to Bernard. We decided our friends had to know him and collect his work, so, in 1987 and in 1998, we hosted an exhibition of his work at our home. And the beat goes on…

We met Jonathan Green in 1988, and had the marvelous pleasure of seeing him work on *Field Hands*, the painting we ultimately acquired. Of course, that made it even more special… I love his "sheets on the line"—that takes me home—as well as his "swing" series. His use of bold, brilliant colors led to other acquisitions and an exhibition at our home to introduce him to friends. One of our Green paintings was selected as a backdrop for the ballet *Off the Wall* that the Charleston Ballet Theater conceived of and toured throughout the South.

And then there's Tina Allen… we always loved her beautiful bronze sculptures and could never decide on which one to acquire until we saw the magnificent *Frederick Douglass*. His elegant, stately presence sat on our dining room table for some time until his pedestal arrived. Imagine having dinner with his piercing eyes watching you! Oh, the stories he could tell… I recently discovered that he spoke in my home town in 1889 before seven hundred people. Tina is gone now, but her presence will always be with us. Her public sculptures of Alex Haley, Martin Luther King, Jr., Tupac Shakur, and many others will educate, inspire, and motivate generations to come.

All of these artists became friends, some before and others after we were proud caretakers of their creative output. Together we have shared many special moments in each others' lives—small personal gatherings, art openings, New Year's celebrations, Fourth of July, birthdays, anniversaries, unveilings, memorials, book signings. These moments have shaped our own history.

Our collecting reflects our self-discovery, our individual and personal history, and memories of growing up in Florida. We have never strayed too far emotionally from those roots. I grew up in St. Augustine, with Mama (my grandmother), and I can now remember her as a collector of sorts. She would quietly and lovingly save swatches of fabric from dresses she made for me and my sister/cousin and other family members. I can remember her piecing those little squares or triangles together for the next quilt she would masterfully make. It was always a treat to try and find "my dress" while the quilting frame was up or after the quilt was finished and on the bed. To this day I have "pieces" done by her as well as some done by my mother as a young woman, before she passed away in 1948 at the age of 21.

My sister Barbara was an art major in college and during the summer she always used me as her model. I would have to sit on the porch rail and not move as she sketched my profile from both sides and all angles. Thus my close relationships with artists began when I was quite young.

My uncle, James A. Webster, who was also my elementary school principal, taught art during the summers at Florida Memorial College, in St. Augustine. There were always paintings in his home, some by him and some by his students. Little did I know at the time that he was friends with Jacob Lawrence, Gwendolyn Knight, Zora Neale Hurston, and Sarah Vaughn.

What a remarkable, creative journey this has been and still is. As we share experiences and information, we learn so much about ourselves. This process of collecting our history evolves and becomes more focused, directed, and intentional, and as it exposes us to new work and new artists, it nourishes our souls.

Bernard and I have been blessed immeasurably, and we encourage those who have joined us on this journey to start their own narrative. Invest time, energy and resources to learn more about our collective history. Invest in an artist when you can, visit museums and become a patron of the arts. Begin your own journey to further educate, inspire, and motivate our young people. Find that special something that catches your eye, captures your heart, and remains in your soul.

— Shirley Pooler Kinsey

Sinalunga, 2001
Carl Anderson
Oil on canvas
20 x 20 in.

Translating Inspiration

My introduction to art, and consequently my passion for it and all things creative, came from my nurturing parents. As far back as I can remember, there were vivid colors and profound words; powerful images and sculpture that seemed like they were larger than life. I remember being drawn to abstract paintings and forming my own interpretations, often letting my imagination run wild. I learned at an early age that art could be used to escape, heal, tell a story, bridge gaps, and inspire. I learned by experiencing all of this, and so much more, firsthand.

I was extremely fortunate to grow up in a household that emphasized education, both formal and nontraditional. Through traveling the world with my parents, I was exposed to the various ways people express themselves and celebrate their cultures, their individuality as well as their similarities. I learned that the world was bigger than my backyard, and that although we may have different approaches, we are far more alike than we are different: we experience the same emotions and desires and are all ultimately searching to live fulfilling lives. As a result of these observations and encounters, I saw that there are many ways to find that fulfillment, and I was fascinated with creative expression as a way not only to become successful but also to love, to give, and to find peace within oneself.

My parents gave me a head start in life by making sure I got a well-rounded view of the world and everything in it. I was often the only kid in a room full of adults, but instead of being forced to act older than my age, I was engaged by the discussions, invited to express what my opinions and interests were, and I felt that those opinions and interests were valued. As my parents became more involved in the art world, I played a part in picking out works and in turn developed my own interest in and passion for art. Some of my favorite artists became like aunts and uncles to me. They took an interest in me and urged me to find my own creative outlets. I grew up surrounded by some of the greatest painters, sculptors, musicians, writers, intellectuals, and corporate moguls of our time—something that has shaped my life and helped make me who I am.

One of those "Uncles" is dear family friend Carl Anderson, a renowned actor and singer. Carl always encouraged me to find my passion and pursue it. He spent a lifetime performing on stages and traveling the world, and he had a confidence and peace about him that I will never forget. That confidence and peace, I always believed, came from his son (also named Khalil), and from doing what he loved. Though he had a well-established singing career over many years, it wasn't until 2001 that Carl was inspired to explore a new passion, for painting. While traveling in Italy with my parents he picked up a canvas and paintbrush and painted his first work, *Sinalunga,* as if it were his calling. There is an African proverb that says, "if you can talk you can sing, if you can walk you can dance," and Carl is a prime example of that, showing that creativity is natural, and that it manifests itself through us in multiple ways.

Although this book is focused on the incredible collection of paintings, sculpture, and historical artifacts that my parents have amassed during a partnership of forty years and more, it is this collection that has given me a profound appreciation for the arts as a whole. Music, dance, poetry, and theater, along with mixed media works, have allowed me to discover myself and my passions. As a teenager I discovered self-expression through poetry/hip-hop, graffiti, dance, and song. It was through my parents' passion that I discovered my own, but it was also through their passion that I discovered my heritage. I've learned so much about African history and the rich culture from which we all come. It made me proud of who I am and showed me that there is so much more to our people than what we learn during Black History Month.

My parents' collection tells the story of the African and African American experience both in the motherland and in the Americas. It shows where we have been and where we are going. It shows our oppression and our victory, our resilience and perseverance, our creativity and our genius. To view the collection and not be overwhelmed with pride is impossible. I am happy that these works are being shared because they are a true educational tool—and even more, in my opinion, they are an inspirational tool.

— Khalil B. Kinsey

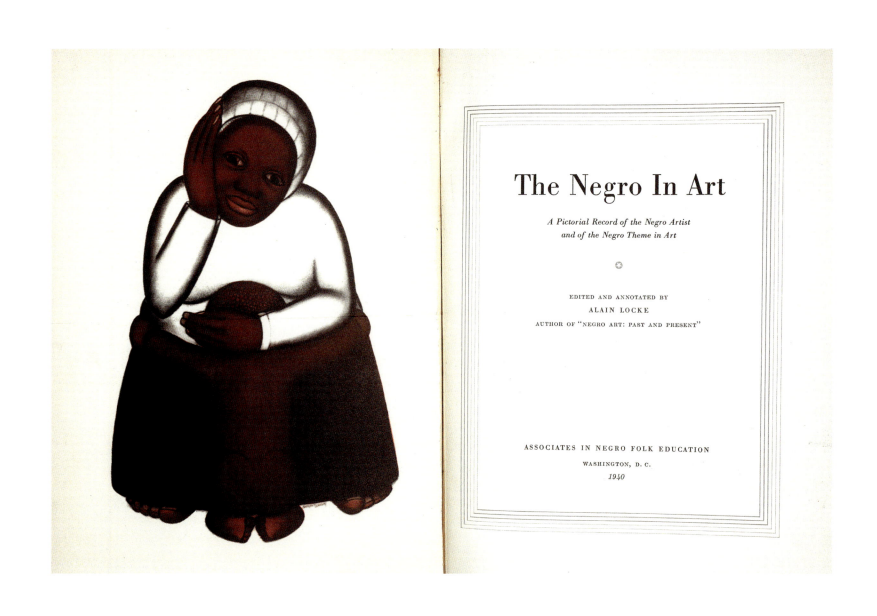

The Negro In Art

*A Pictorial Record of the Negro Artist
and of the Negro Theme in Art*

✦

EDITED AND ANNOTATED BY
ALAIN LOCKE
AUTHOR OF "NEGRO ART: PAST AND PRESENT"

ASSOCIATES IN NEGRO FOLK EDUCATION
WASHINGTON, D. C.
1940

The Negro in Art, 1941
Alain Locke
Book
12 ¼ x 9 ¼ x 1 in.

The Birth of an Aesthetic

The pulse of the Negro world has begun to beat in Harlem.

— Alain Locke

The power of the Kinsey Collection lies in the representation of cultural cross-pollination. The most visually compelling era for these influences was the early 20th century, when a movement was underway in Harlem, at Howard University and Dunbar High in Washington, D.C., and in urban centers throughout the United States. Artists, writers, poets, actors, musicians, and scholars came together to immerse themselves in a new discourse on identity, and a black renaissance was born. The Harlem Renaissance centered on the idea that black artists should not have to follow the canon of western art, literature, and music, but could establish their own aesthetic, interpreting the world around them in a uniquely African American way.

During this time, many artists and scholars, among them W. E. B. DuBois, Alain Locke, and Carter G. Woodson, who had an assertive and celebratory approach to discussing and promulgating black culture, began to call for a more visible and more definitive voice. Many artists answered the call, and then reached out to the younger generation to ensure that the momentum of the movement was sustainable.

They became teachers—notably among them Aaron Douglas and Augusta Savage, who helped spread a new black paradigm across the country and around the world.

Bernard Kinsey is extremely interested in Americans and others who recognized black brilliance. While the birth of a profound black aesthetic was supported by many, one man in particular piques Kinsey's interest: Julius Rosenwald. In 1917, Rosenwald, President of Sears, Roebuck and Co., established the Julius Rosenwald Fund to support the most pressing issues of the day: racial inequality and black mobility. He donated over $60 million to African American social, educational, and cultural initiatives. From 1928 to 1948, the fund awarded stipends to hundreds of prominent and emerging African American artists, writers, and scholars, including DuBois, Ralph Ellison, Zora Neale Hurston, Elizabeth Catlett, Eldzier Cortor, Aaron Douglas, Katherine Dunham, Jacob Lawrence, Gordon Parks, Marion Perkins, Augusta Savage, Charles White, and Hale Woodruff.

Another major, though unlikely, supporter of the Harlem Renaissance was a white real estate developer, William Harmon. He established the Harmon Foundation to celebrate black achievement in the arts and sciences. The foundation sponsored competitions to encourage artists nationwide to join those in Harlem who were creating this new, strong vision of black identity.

One Harmon Foundation winner was Hale Woodruff, the first African American to attend Indiana University's prestigious Herron Art School. Other foundation award recipients include Palmer Hayden, Charles Alston, and Aaron Douglas. The Kinseys collect these renowned artists, as well as the Harmon Foundation catalogues that played such an important role in the artists' national and international success. They view these documents as a testament to their own goal of cultivation: recognizing greatness, fostering and sharing it with people who want to broaden their knowledge and understanding of the world around them.

Others involved in the production and promotion of the African American artistic tradition worked at a grass roots level to ensure that artists had venues to present their work. James Herring, founder of Howard University's department of art, and Alonzo Aden, curator of the university's art gallery, founded a private gallery in their Washington, D.C., home, collecting works by African American artists who are featured in the Kinsey Collection. Herring and Aden supported the artists who inspired a movement, and they built the first African American gallery, which became the Barnett-Aden Collection.

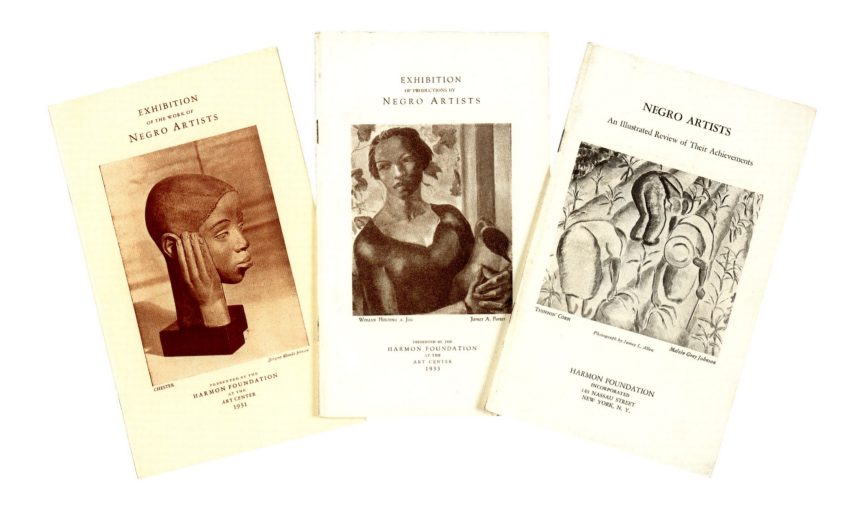

Exhibition of the Work of Negro Artists, 1931
  Harmon Foundation
  Exhibition catalogue
  8 x 5 in.

Exhibition of the Productions by Negro Artists, 1933
  Harmon Foundation
  Exhibition catalogue
  8 x 5 in.

Negro Artists: An Illustrated Review of Their Achievements, 1935
  Harmon Foundation
  Exhibition catalogue
  8 x 5 in.

Westchester County, 1935
Palmer Hayden
Oil on canvas
18 x 24 in.

Ping Pong, 1934
Allan Rohan Crite
Graphite on paper
21 ½ x 19 in.

Boy's Head, 1931
James Lesesne Wells
Linocut
19 ¼ x 15 ½ in.

Georgia Youth, 1934
Hale Woodruff
Linocut
17 x 13 ¼ in.

Portrait of Girl, 1940
Charles Alston
Oil on canvas
28 ½ x 24 ¾ in.

200 Year Old Tree, 2004

Edward Loper

Oil on canvas

30 x 36 in.

River Landscape, 1940
John Wesley Hardwick
Oil on board
24 x 34 in.

The Farm House, 1942
Dox Thrash
Pen and ink on paper
9 x 6 in.

African Women, 1942
Eldzier Cortor
Pen and ink on woven paper
16 x 11 ½ in.

Five Letters, 1942–1943
Zora Neale Hurston
Ink on paper
Various sizes

Shirley Kinsey discovered these letters among her uncle's papers after his death in 1993. James A. Webster, her uncle, had befriended many artists and scholars of the Harlem Renaissance while he was a student at Columbia University. He established a deep friendship with the writer and anthropologist Zora Neale Hurston, who was also from Florida. They continued their friendship after university, spending time together in St. Augustine, where Webster was a professor at Florida Memorial College. In 1960, a St. Augustine elementary school was named in honor of his contributions to teaching. Hurston was raised in Eatonville, Florida, one of the first all-black towns to be formed after the Emancipation Proclamation in 1863, and in 1887 it was the first such town to be incorporated. Her novel *Their Eyes Were Watching God* (1937) provides a brief overview of the founding of the town through the eyes of Janie Crawford, the main character.

The Kinseys have two other Hurston books in their collection, *Jonah's Gourd Vine* and *Tell My Horse*. The later is signed and inscribed to Shirley's uncle, "To "Dick" Webster With that old–time feeling."

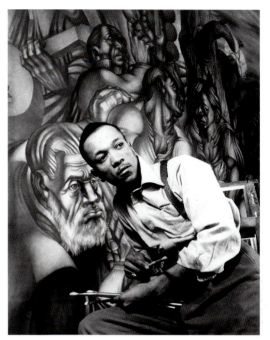

Charles White, 1943
Gordon Parks
Gelatin silver print
8 x 10 in.

The Couple, 1940
Charles White
Ink on paper
18 x 14 in.

**The Dreamer, a Portrait of
Dorothy Dandridge,** 1951
Charles White
Ink on paper
16 ½ x 24 in.

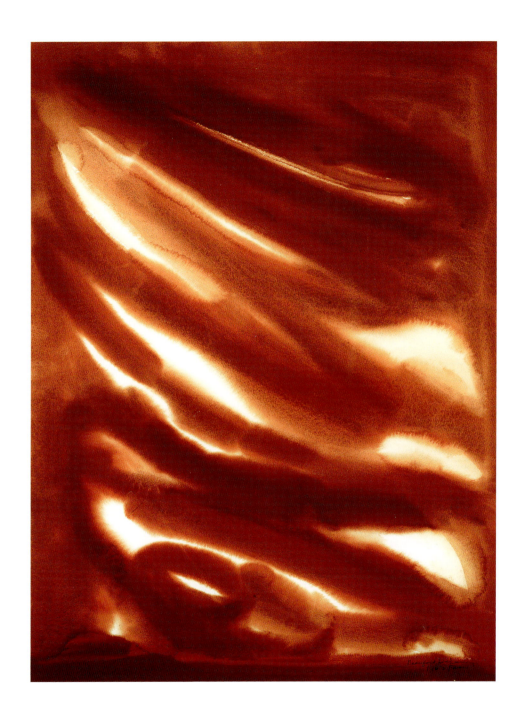

Paris, 1963
Beauford Delaney
Oil on woven paper
25 x 19 ½ in.

European Influences

The understanding of art depends finally upon one's willingness to extend one's humanity and one's knowledge of human life.

— Ralph Ellison

As noted previously, Europe was the site of many of the historical and artistic intersections that inspire the Kinseys to collect. Surprising and important vignettes come into focus through items in their collection, including Pope Clement VII's protection of Leo Africanus and Robert Scott Duncanson's privileged upbringing with his father in Scotland. These individuals contributed to the cultural movements that would transform artistic and intellectual canons. During the world wars, however, cultural intersections like these took place more broadly, as a large number of African Americans shared their cultural traditions with their European hosts. An African American aesthetic infused with a globalizing perspective now added to the complexity of black American identity.

Henry O. Tanner, whose work is represented in the Kinsey Collection, left the United States to begin a thriving career in Paris, where he lived until his death in 1937. He hosted and befriended scores of black artists and scholars, including Alain Locke, Augusta Savage, Hale Woodruff, and his best friend in Paris, Palmer Hayden. These artists grappled with the tension in America between black ideals and white realities, between living as artists and acting as insurgents against the aggressive and powerful enemy, racism. They met to create and to discuss their ideas, and to mourn the intractability of discrimination.

But in Europe, they also fell in love. In Paris, the city of lights, they fell in love with the skyline and landscape, but also with its openness to black thinkers, who needed space to confront profound problems. That love is reflected in the work of many black artists whose aesthetic sensibilities reflect their complex position as "others," both in Europe and in America.

Almost every artist who came of age during the Harlem Renaissance traveled to Europe. Some received Harmon Foundation awards for study in Paris. Many artists, including Richmond Barthé, Lois Mailou Jones, and Beauford Delaney, were invigorated in Europe and then returned to the United States to continue their work, despite harsh environments. Others became true expatriates and lived for the rest of their lives in Europe. The work of these artists was enriched by both worlds.

The Dancer, 1937
Richmond Barthé
Bronze
17 x 8 x 7 in.

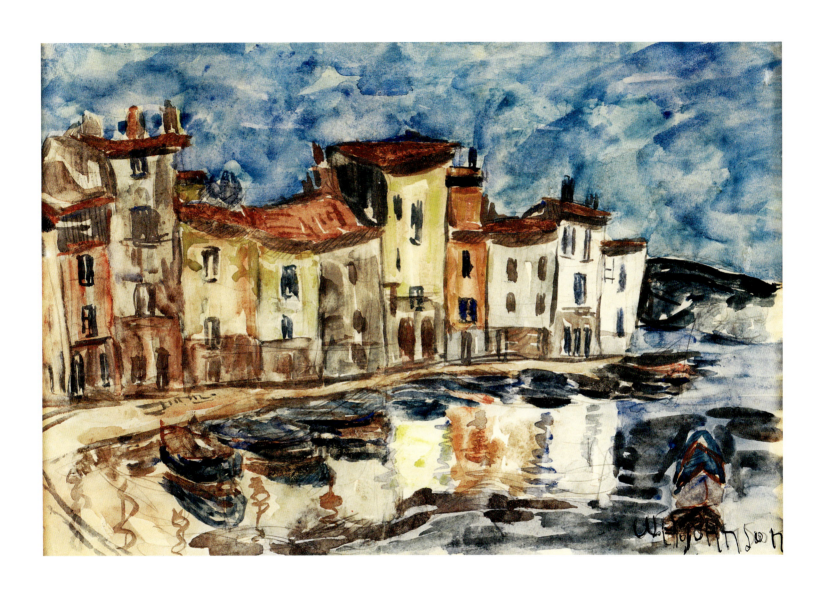

Martigues Coastal Scene, 1932
William H. Johnson
Watercolor
20 ½ x 26 ¾ x 2 in.

Child's Play, 1950
Aaron Douglas
Watercolor
11 ¾ x 8 ½ in.

Self Portrait, 1931
James Porter
Charcoal pencil on paper
24 x 20 ¼ in.

Gusting Up to 35, 1972
Palmer Hayden
Oil on board
36 x 28 in.

A New Generation of Masters

Art is not simply works of art; it is the spirit that knows beauty; that has music in its soul and the color of the sunset in its handkerchief, that can dance on a flaming world and make the world dance too.

— W. E. B. DuBois

Bernard and Shirley Kinsey's collection strongly represents artists who were the progeny of the Harlem Renaissance masters. This second generation followed their mentors' example, conjoining formal education with unique points of view from African American culture. These artists are of particular importance not only for their technical and cultural contributions but also because they were the first to be truly integrated into modern American art culture.

Jacob Lawrence captured the imagination of a nation with his profound and haunting renderings of the African American life he saw growing up in Harlem. He employed bold color in a decisively new style. Lawrence was the first African American artist to be elected a member of the National Institute of Arts and Letters and the first black president of the organization.

Norman Lewis was elected the first president of the Spiral Group, which sought to advance the goals of the civil rights movement through the visual arts. Although his early work was grounded in social realism, he later worked beside Willem de Kooning, Jackson Pollack, and Mark Rothko in the abstract expressionist movement born in New York in the 1950s. Since his death in 1979, he has assumed a major place in histories of American art and has been featured in several important exhibits.

Bob Blackburn's printmaking workshop in Chelsea Village, Manhattan, established him as both an American print master and one of the most generous artists of his time. Artists from all walks of life, including Robert Rauschenberg and Roy DeCarava, worked with Blackburn in his workshop and went on to critical acclaim around the world. Blackburn's altruism and dedication to community coincide with the very best of what the Kinsey Collection represents, values shared by many of the artists and contributors to the collection.

Encouraged by artist Alma Thomas, a young Sam Gilliam extended the possibilities of modern art with innovative abstract works on different media, including loose, draped canvas, wood, and steel. Today, Gilliam is internationally known as the premier African American painter of "color-field" works, large canvases usually occupied by a single block of color, the successor to abstract expressionism as a dominant form.

The youngest artist to exhibit at the 1962 Seattle World's Fair, which included a major international survey of modern art, Chicagoan Richard Hunt has garnered national attention for his sculpture, which exists mainly as public art around the country. His work is also in the permanent collection of the Museum of Modern Art in New York.

John Brown Series, #8, 1977
Jacob Lawrence
Serigraph
22 ½ x 28 ¼ in.

Falling Star, 1979
Romare Bearden
Lithograph
34 ½ x 29 in.

Untitled

"To Rosalie and Robert [Gwathmey] for Great Summers,"

1977

Norman Lewis

Oil on paper

38 x 31 ¾ in.

Untitled, 1960
Bob Blackburn
Lithograph
29 x 34 in.

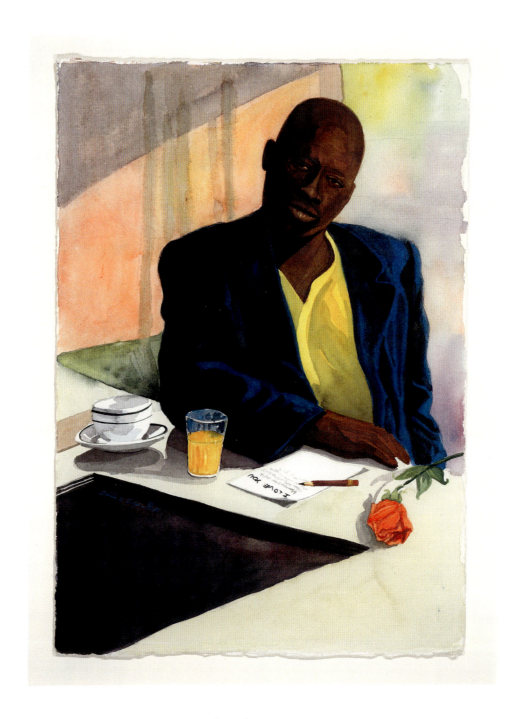

Love Letter, 1995
Dane Tilghman
Watercolor on paper
20 ½ x 14 ¾ in.

Ka'ena Point, 2009
Keith Morris Washington
Oil on panel
6 x 20 in.

Wonder, 2005
Sam Gilliam
Mixed media
40 x 44 x 4 in.

Inside Out Series, ca. 1986
Richard Hunt
Cast bronze
13 ¾ x 13 x 12 in.

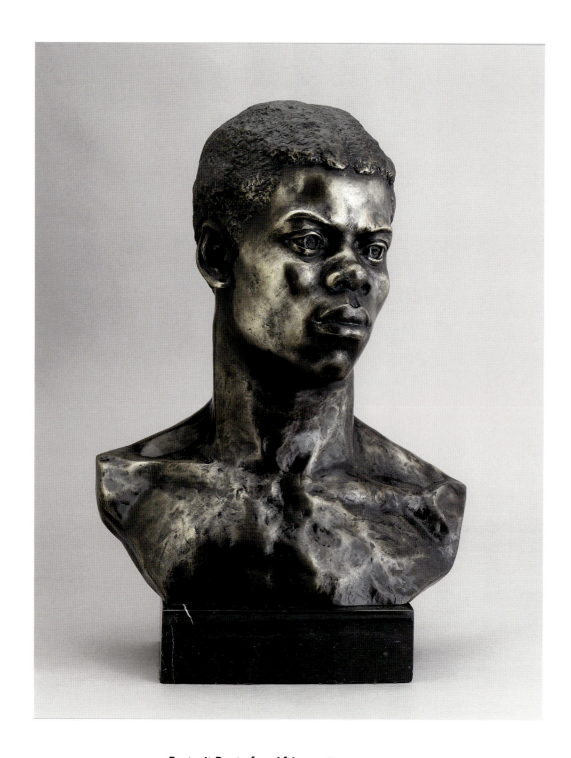

Portrait Bust of an African, 1899–1900
May Howard Jackson
Bronze
21 x 12 ¾ in.

African American Women in the Arts

I think I'm just lucky at a time when it's fashionable or it's necessary to do something about a black woman.

— Elizabeth Catlett

One of the things that most attracted Bernard and Shirley Kinsey to the work of the early African American masters (featured in the "Early Genius" section of this catalogue) was that these painters succeeded as professional artists while the majority of African Americans were still enslaved. The five artists featured in that section were instrumental in establishing an American aesthetic in the 19th century. The artists of the Harlem Renaissance and the broader Negritude Movement further contributed to that aesthetic, redefining the notion of the primitive in modern art and working in a wide variety of media and genres, including literature and music as well as visual art.

The early masters and others featured in the preceding pages were not the only artists to gain praise and recognition during the 20th century. Black women artists proved their talents through technical skill and aesthetic daring, challenging conventions and experimenting in various media and styles. These innovators hold a special place in the lexicon of African American artists, and the Kinseys have singled out some of those who have made the load lighter and the road more interesting to travel.

May Howard Jackson's *Portrait Bust of an African* serves as a visual reminder of the transatlantic slave trade for Bernard, and it is one of his most valued works. Jackson was influential in American sculpture and African American artistic pedagogy. Born to a middle-class family in Philadelphia, she was the first African American woman to attend the Pennsylvania Academy of the Fine Arts, where she was enrolled from 1895 to 1898 and again from 1900 to 1902. She was mentored by pioneer African American sculptor Meta Warrick Fuller, but decided against following Fuller to Paris to continue her studies. Instead, Jackson married, settled in Washington, D.C., and became a mentor and instructor to many prolific black artists of the 20th century, including her husband's nephew, Sargent Johnson, and James Porter.

Laura Wheeler Waring also attended the Pennsylvania Academy of the Fine Arts, beginning in 1908. She was a prominent portrait artist whose works were exhibited in museums around the world. Waring was commissioned to paint the Harmon Foundation's series "Portraits of Outstanding American Citizens of Negro Origin," which included the now famous portraits of W. E. B. Dubois and Marian Anderson.

The Kinseys are stewards of a beautiful rendering of quotidian existence painted by one of the most widely recognized women artists, Lois Mailou Jones. Born in Boston in 1905, Jones was also mentored by Meta Fuller and attended the Designers Art School of Boston and later the Acadèmie Julien in Paris. She was a teacher and prolific artist at Howard University, earning recognition from President Jimmy Carter at the White House in 1980.

Born in Georgia in 1891, Alma Thomas and her family moved to Washington, D.C., after the 1906 race riots. Thomas became an art teacher in the public school system and studied design at Howard University. After joining Jones' Little Paris group of artists, Thomas was introduced to abstract expressionism, which changed her life and her art forever. While abstract, her work is alive with emotion and color.

Another Jones student at Howard was Elizabeth Catlett, who fell in love with sculpture and the work of Mexican muralists under the tutelage of James Porter. Later, Catlett earned the first master's degree awarded in fine arts at the State University of Iowa. She won a Rosenwald fellowship in 1946 and traveled to Mexico, where she was befriended by Diego Rivera, Rufino Tamayo, and Francisco Mora (whom she later married). Catlett, who still lives in Mexico, continues to be one of America's most renowned sculptors.

Woman, 1989
Artis Lane
Bronze sculpture
31 x 15 ½ x 8.0 in.

Classic Head 1, 1994
Artis Lane
Bronze sculpture
16 ½ x 8 ½ x 9.0 in.

Mr. Bernard Kinsey, 2004
Buena Johnson
Watercolor, pencil, collage
20 x 16 in.

Family, 1928
Laura Wheeler Waring
Oil on board
8 x 8 in.

Fishermen, Fishing Boats and Women Sketching, 1947
Lois Mailou Jones
Watercolor
29 ¼ x 34 ¼ in.

Fiery Sunset, 1973
Alma Thomas
Acrylic on canvas
41 ¼ x 41 in.

Jackie, 1974
Elizabeth Catlett
Lithograph
34 x 27 in.

Untitled, ca. 1980
Elizabeth Catlett
Bronze sculpture
19 x 9 x 6 in.

The Faces of My People, 1990
Margaret Burroughs
Woodcut
28 x 32 ¾ in.

As Violence, 1973
Phoebe Beasley
Watercolor on paper
20 ½ x 28 ½ in.

Piano, Bass and Drums, 2000
Phoebe Beasley
Mixed media
25 ½ x 25 ½ in.

Shirley at Sixty, 2006
Phoebe Beasley
Mixed media
20 x 24 in.

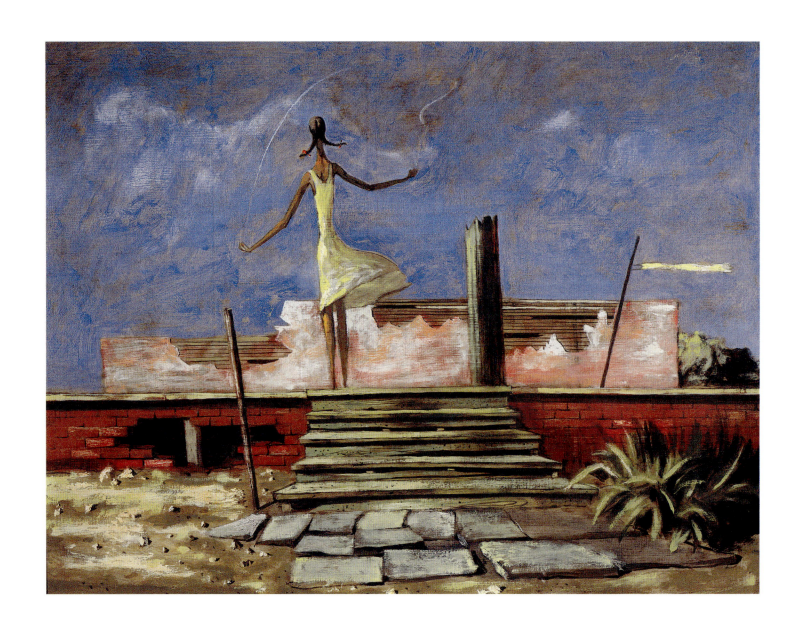

Untitled, 1951

Hughie Lee-Smith

Oil on masonite

18 x 24 in.

Southern Home

In every conceivable manner, the family is link to our past, bridge to our future.

— Alex Haley

Much of what Bernard and Shirley Kinsey have collected is intended to ground them in their personal history as well as that of the broader African American experience. Bernard is driven to capture the intersections between history and culture. When considering the visual arts, Shirley Kinsey's goals are similar but more subjective. She often chooses work that reminds her of their Southern upbringing and brings to light the best aspects of Florida and the South's conflicted past. Shirley always chooses celebratory images that reflect her recollections of a powerful yet loving grandmother and a supportive extended family.

The works in this section thus depict Southern black life in ways that speak directly to the Kinseys' cherished memories. For Shirley, the young pig-tailed girl in Hughie Lee-Smith's work is a reflection of her young self, playing under the southern sun, lively and aware but carefree and whole. This is the space where her dreams of mobility and the dedication to social justice began.

Claude Clark's *Guest House* reminds Shirley of her grandmother's home off a dirt road in St. Augustine, Florida. These pieces, along with Jonathan Green's depictions of the women workers, serve as markers of the past that have nourished the Kinseys and encouraged them to undertake and continue their remarkable journey through life together, and to the 90 countries they have now visited.

Bernard and Shirley Kinsey always loved to travel, and later they began to document their expeditions with photographs. Now they collect the masters. When they come home to California, however, they return to that fundamental part of themselves represented by the artwork that is their Southern home.

Guest House, 1950
Claude Clark
Oil on board
16 x 20 in.

Field Hands, 1988
Jonathan Green
Oil on masonite
37 ¼ x 29 ¼ in.

Farmer's Wife, ca. 1954

Robert Gwathmey

Color serigraph

17 x 13 ¼ in.

Farm Boy, 1990
William Tolliver
Sand on linocut
40 ½ x 30 ½ in.

Kenyatta Center, Nairobi, Kenya
Harambi Street, 1987-1991
John Biggers
Pen and pencil on paper
10 ¼ x 20 ¼ in.

African American Artists of the West

Art is the only thing you cannot punch a button for. You must do it the old-fashioned way. Stay up and really burn the midnight oil. There are no compromises.

— Leontyne Price

Bernard and Shirley Kinsey moved to Los Angeles in 1967 and bought their first house in 1971. Their son Khalil was born soon after. As their careers flourished, so did their disposable income, much of which they saved. However, early in their marriage they discovered the joy of collecting art and artifacts, which helped them document their lives together and also served as reminders of their beginnings, goals, and dreams.

Through hard work, determination, and strong faith, Bernard and Shirley Kinsey prospered and found themselves looking backward, seeking to coalesce their experiences, travels, and memories through their collection. Now surrounded by ocean vistas and canyon landscapes, the Kinseys have embraced their adopted Southern California home and have forged a special bond with black artists whose lives and work in the West resonate with their spirit.

African Americans have long been able to explore their creativity in the West, but often without the recognition they deserve. A 1933 Harmon Foundation catalogue claimed that Sargent Johnson was the only recognized African American artist in California. Johnson, like Grafton Tyler Brown before him, skillfully melded craft and fine art. By the time that Thelma Johnson Streat joined Johnson on Works Progress Administration projects in the Bay Area, African American heritage was recognized as a primary source for realizing a middle ground in the debate between high and low culture. California gave black artists the freedom to investigate the relationship between their identity and their art.

Throughout the 20th century, black artists in California continued to challenge conventional notions of fine art and evolve new ones. The assemblage movement of the 1960s placed California artists such as Betye Saar, David Hammonds, and Noah Purifoy on the international stage. Artists active in the West, notably Charles White, created a distinctive representation of black experience in America and new art forms. They inspired a generation of African American artists to explore the cultural and visual landscape of the region, producing work richly layered with meaning.

The Kinseys have personally met many artists represented in their collection, through travel in the West and through California gallery owners, Thelma Harris and Alitash Kebede. Kebede introduced them to William Pajaud, among others, who motivated Shirley to champion living black artists whenever she could. They met John Biggers, who has fostered the success of many African American art students, as have a number of artists represented in the Kinsey Collection. The Kinseys commissioned John Biggers to travel to Kenya for the painting pictured on the opposite page, which was then given as a gift to Florida A&M. The artists represented in the following pages are living, working, or were trained in California, Colorado, Texas, and throughout the West.

Fugue, 2000
Richard Mayhew
Oil on canvas
55 ½ x 51 ½ in.

Seascape, 1984
William Pajaud
Watercolor
31 x 41 in.

Old Maasai Woman, 1986
Ed Dwight
Bronze
38 x 14 x 10 ½ in.

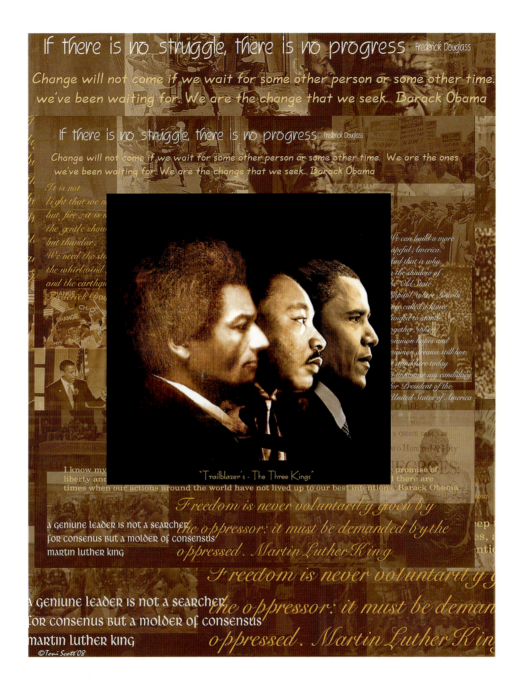

"Trailblazer's - The Three Kings"

"Trailblazer's - The Three Kings," 2008
Toni Scott
Mixed media on paper
22 x 17 in.

Blue Jazz, 1994
Bill Dallas
Oil on board
49 x 37 in.

***Absorption I, III, IV*, 1987**
Matthew Thomas
Clay and acrylic on plywood
84 x 42 x 2 ½ in.

Landscape, 1995
Dr. Samella Lewis
Signed serigraph 1/60
28 x 23 in.

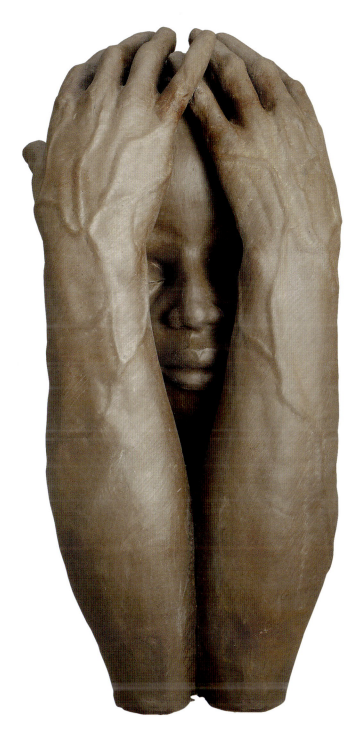

***Loss,* 1998**
Michael Chukes
Clay sculpture
16 x 8 x 9 in.

The Beach Runner, 1997
Ernie Barnes
Acrylic on paper
27 x 37 in.

Slow Drag, 1997
Ernie Barnes
Acrylic on paper
38 x 35 in.

Paris Revisited, 2002
Alonzo Davis
Mixed media
Acrylic, Bamboo & Wood
19 x 51 x 6 in.

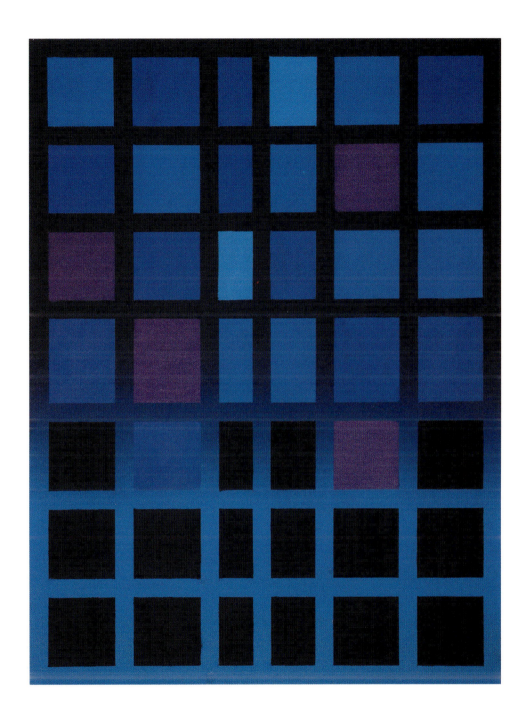

Étude 17 en Couleur, 2002
Ed Pratt
Oil on canvas
24 x 18 in.

Heart to Heart, 1996
Lionel Lofton
Lithograph
17 x 21 in.

The Gambler, 1990
William Sylvester Carter
Oil on canvas
18 ½ x 16 ½ in.

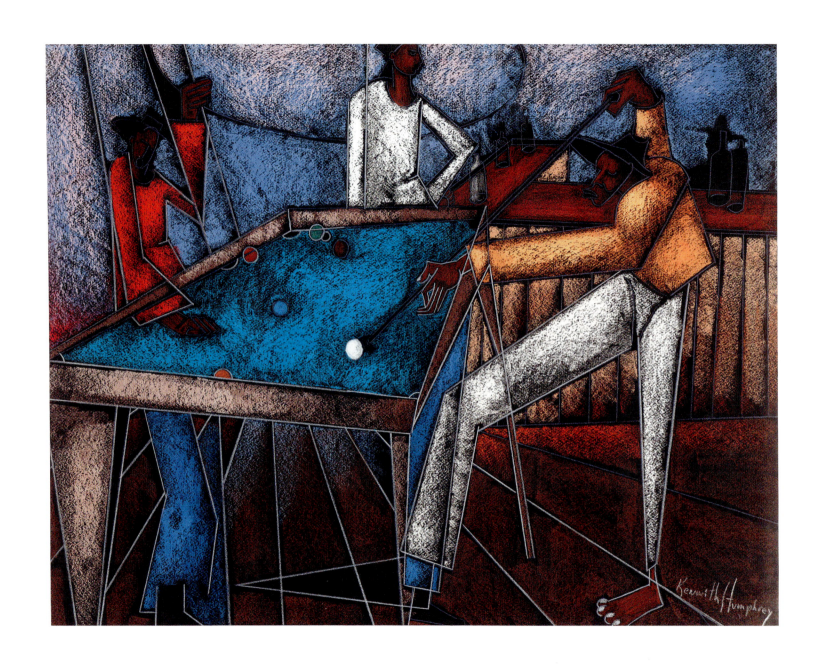

Mississippi Pool Hall, 2000

Kennith Humphrey

Acrylic on canvas

20 x 20 ½ in.

Untitled, 1992

Kadir Nelson

Serigraph

34 x 21 ½ in.

Unknown, 2001
Ricardo Losada
Oil on board
25 x 19 in.

The Americas + 1

Travel has been a big part of our lives since the beginning of our marriage. Our first trip, to the Grand Canyon, led to further exploration in the southwest that was the beginning of our appreciation for Native American culture. We decided to explore all of the national parks of the West, and soon we realized that we had visited forty-three. We then began to spread our wings, and we visited the other Americas: South and Central America and the Caribbean islands. One of our first trips out of the U.S. was a three-week journey to South America in 1976. There we saw Machu Picchu, Iguazu Falls, Rio de Janeiro, the Amazon, Chile, Columbia, and Argentina. Each time we return home after experiencing other cultures, our desire to discover more about our own is heightened.

Early on we began looking for art on our travels and have discovered some wonderful images. One of our favorite pieces is a painting by Belizean artist Papo that we call Middle Street, San Pedro Town, Ambergris Caye. On a trip to Cuba we were introduced to an artist named Ricardo Losado, who depicts the Cuban landscape and experience, that draws you into the scene. During that same visit to Cuba, we had the opportunity to meet Fidel Castro.

Works of art have also marked personal milestones and relationships for us. On my fortieth birthday, my close friend and mentor Guy Dobbs, a vice president of a major Xerox division in the 1980s, gave me a painting by Brazilian artist Terciliano Jr. (pictured on page 152.) The great talent Carl Anderson, also a very close friend, gave us the beautiful Haitian Vodou flag by Maxon Scylla.

Although this chapter is devoted to the Americas, we wanted to include one of Shirley's favorite genres of art, Australian Aboriginal dot painting. We have traveled to Australia twice and have fallen in love with the Aboriginal culture and artwork. The Aboriginal story is similar to the story of Native Americans: conquest, massacre, and forced acculturation. But through this long ordeal they have maintained their cultural practices. Aboriginal paintings are based on the myth of the Dreamtime, which dates back over 40,000 years to some of the oldest rock paintings in the world. The piece that we are highlighting is an oil painting, Bush Plum by Colin Bird, which we pur-chased in 1996. The bush plum, which grows less than three feet high, is used for "smoke medicine" —the ancient holistic medical beliefs practiced by the Aboriginal people that recognizes the social, physical and spiritual dimensions of health and life.

The African American poet Langston Hughes gives voice to these themes in "Let America be America Again" (circa 1930's)

"O, let America be America again—
The land that never has been yet—
And yet must be—the land where every man is free.
The land that's mine—the poor man's,
Indian's, Negro's, ME—
Who made America,
Whose sweat and blood, whose faith and pain,
Whose hand at the foundry, whose plow in the rain,
Must bring back our mighty dream again."

"O, yes,
I say it plain,
America never was America to me,
And yet I swear this oath—America will be!"

Middle Street San Pedro Town, Ambergris Caye,

2001

Eduardo "Papo" Alamilla

Oil on canvas

32 x 38 in.

Haitian Voodoo Flag, ca. 1990
Maxon Scylla
Mixed media
beads, sequins, on fabric
36 ½ x 30 in.

Brazilian Abstract, 1984
Terciliano Jr.
Oil on canvas
15 ¼ x 23 ¼ in.

Bush Plum / Dot Painting, 1996
Colin Bird
Oil on canvas
41 ¾ x 46 in.

Living with Art

People collect art and artifacts for many different reasons. Some are aesthetes who aim to capture moments of beauty; others collect to possess, to own a body of work or a body of ideas. Like many collectors, Bernard and Shirley Kinsey began collecting objects and art to document their lives, as a way to reflect on their maturation as people, as parents, and as professionals.

Bernard, as an executive at Xerox, gave prints of *High Aspirations* by Ernie Barnes to top performing sales people. His intention was both to honor and to educate his staff while bridging cultural differences, and to forge connections through mutual aesthetic appreciation. The Kinseys also collected art during their travels around the world, on their quest for knowledge of things larger than themselves. These beginnings evolved into a passion that became its own journey: to discover who and what came

before them, and what could propel them further along their path. As the Kinseys identified themes emerging from their collection, they began to shape a larger purpose for the art and artifacts in their possession: to inspire and educate others through a repository of culturally important material.

The Kinseys' vision—to document the past and the present through the collection of historical documents, and two- and three-

family in the twilight years of life. But all who visit experience similar feelings of wonder and astonishment at the perseverance and hope that shines through these artifacts.

The Kinseys are continually educating themselves as well as their guests about what it means to be stewards of such a powerful legacy. They feel grounded by this work, surrounded by the accomplishments of generations who were without resources or protection. Their home is a vivid reminder of all those who forged the path to freedom. What could then be achieved along that path becomes apparent on the walls: the sheer number of artists and ephemera bears witness to an enormous variety of artistic expression across eras and continents. It is impressive, and humbling.

The weight of this ongoing interaction with history is lightened by the design of the house, constructed to showcase the collection. Light from floor-to-ceiling windows fills the house, with views onto the gleaming Pacific and the hillsides of Pacific Palisades. The design merges inside and outside, and this theme reflects the way in which the Kinseys live with art and cultural objects. A Dogon ladder from Mali greets visitors outside the front door, a natural composition based on their deep appreciation for their African roots. Inside the door, a seven-foot sculpture by California artist Matthew Thomas with elements of African ritualized carving, Native American symbolism, and Buddhist energy welcomes all visitors. It encourages an exploration of the intersections of space and place that signify the Kinseys' passion for life and collecting in a global context.

Everywhere in the Kinsey home, on all the walls and surfaces, one finds art from the far corners of the world. There are carved images from Northwest Coast Indian tribes and an Inuit polar bear carved from walrus tusk. A large painting, *The 200 Year Old Tree* by Ed Loper, stands as sentinel opposite an "ethnic wall" that includes African ritual masks, a beautifully woven breastplate from Papua New Guinea, and Kachina Dolls from the Hopi in Arizona. Each artifact carries equal merit and is linked to a personal story. Often, close by, one can find a book detailing work similar to that on display, such as George Swinton's *Sculptures of the Eskimo* (1972), as evidence of the Kinseys' quest to educate themselves about the contexts of these remarkably diverse works.

The art and artifacts that comprise the Kinsey Collection are varied, yet speak a single story. A narrative emerges—from the striking face of the Haida carving, to the Steuben crystal with sculptural elements that complement the fine art around it, to the technically masterful Chinese jade sculptures and the large abstract

Haida Indian Mask

dimensional art—requires an ongoing process of discovery. It also requires tenacity and courage, particularly because the collection contains many grim reminders of the subjugation of black people and black identity.

Bernard and Shirley Kinsey find that leading people down to the "history gallery" in their home is like taking them on a journey through time. Guests range in age from their son Khalil's young friends to artists, friends, and

Inuit Mother and Child, 1975
fossilized whale bone

paintings by Bill Dallas, harmoniously juxtaposed to Aboriginal dot paintings. Each object and work of art is infused with the Kinseys' own story as a couple, yet they are also individuals with different interests that sometimes intersect, sometimes diverge. Bernard says that he collected the early African American masters less for aesthetic reasons than for the historical interest and importance of art made by blacks at a time when most were enslaved. Shirley, however, has a strong connection with the rich colors and the brushstrokes that bring to life bucolic scenes mindful of her childhood in Florida, and of African American life in the South. She seeks visual reminders of her past, to sustain her in the face of the materialism of life in Los Angeles.

Bernard's greatest passion is his love for Shirley; therefore, he, too, is made whole by reminders of her past. Together, they can recount their journeys to over 90 countries through the images and artifacts they have collected. There are stories of Bernard's passion for polar bears, of Shirley's response to streets in the Caribbean that reminded her so much of her childhood neighborhood, of their interactions with people in various parts of the world, who greeted them with great appreciation of their generosity and their willingness to travel long distances to learn about different cultures.

Bernard and Shirley's story includes people who share their passion, and have contributed to the collection through gifts. The Malawi chief's chair, with intricately carved figures in relief, was a gift from the Xerox Black Employees Association in gratitude for Bernard's leadership. Their portrait by California artist and friend Artis Lane was another gift from generous friends. Lane's sculptures are prominent in the Kinsey home, alongside her portrait of Khalil.

Images of the Kinseys created by both famous and emerging artists can be found throughout their home. They are modest about these pieces, although it is clear that they hold a special place in their hearts. Shirley is constantly discovering new ways of seeing, through her interactions with artists such as Phoebe Beasley, Bill Pajaud, Richard Mayhew, and Ed Dwight. These encounters extend her awareness and push her to explore new media.

For Bernard, much of the power of collecting lies in the tangibility of objects: holding

Equiano's 18th-century writings in his hand; studying at the source and expand his understanding of the cultural capital he shares with the world through the exhibition, "The Kinsey Collection: Shared Treasures of Bernard and Shirley Kinsey," and publications highlighting the collection.

Bernard and Shirley share deep intellectual curiosity and hunger for exploration, and a profound commitment to their mission as both cultivators of knowledge and stewards of history. Their home is a testimony to their passion for this commitment, and is in itself a work of art.

Living with such a large and provocative collection of art and history has obvious benefits

Hopi Kachina Doll

left: **Young Maasai Woman,** Ed Dwight   right: **The Pipers,** Ed Dwight

for the Kinseys, but the advantages for visitors who encounter the collection are also extraordinary. Those who see it there or in museums across America have had the opportunity to join them as stewards of a remarkable past of perseverance and accomplishment, and of a vibrant present filled with beauty and variety. The Kinseys' daily interaction with such inspiration ensures that many more will share in their legacy.

Cactus Flower Breastplate
Papua New Guinea

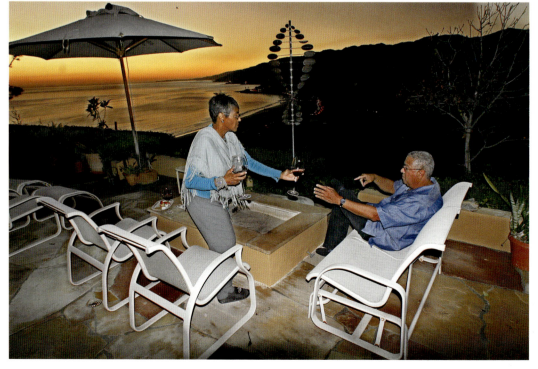

Artists' Biographies

Eduardo "Papo" Alamilla (1965–)

Born on the Island of San Pedro, Belize, Eduardo Alamilla, better known as "Papo", began painting as a young boy. Papo is a humble man, who feels he inherited his grandmother's painting talent. Papo calls his style "realism". He depicts history, scenes, and stories of the people, culture, lifestyle, and mood of Belize. Although he never attended art school, he is studied by many artists and passes his ability on to others. Papo is considered the pride of San Pedro, Ambergris Caye, Belize.

Mikel Alatza (1954–)

Alatza grew up in Fort Wayne, Indiana, where his mother was a social worker and his father a commercial illustrator. He moved to Los Angeles in 1975. A late bloomer, he started painting at 35, essentially self-taught, although his work reflects his father's penchant for detail. His unique approach to portraiture developed through a series of mistakes and experiments. His portraits progressed into three-dimensional objects, and he began experimenting by connecting steel pipes to the sides of stretcher bars, allowing cutout plywood images to be suspended above images in the background. As he matured, his portraits have become both more streamlined and more personalized. Design has become a key aspect of his work, merging technical prowess and aesthetic vision in the creation of truly unique portraits.

Tina Allen (1955–2008)

Born in 1955, in Hempstead, New York, Allen was mentored by sculptor William Zorach and attended Pratt Institute and the New York School of Visual Arts. She also studied art at the University of South Alabama. In 1986, Allen won a competition for a commission to create a memorial statue of African American labor activist A. Philip Randolph, who founded a union for train porters in 1925. Allen has created memorial statues of distinguished Africans and African Americans, including Malcolm X and Nelson Mandela.

Charles Alston (1907–1977)

Alston earned bachelor's and master's degrees from Columbia University. Like many of his contemporaries, including Augusta Savage, he was both artist and educator, teaching many of the most talented African American artists of the 20th century, such as Jacob Lawrence and Romare Bearden. Alston was influenced by ritual African art as well as Mexican muralists Diego Rivera and Jose Clemente Orozco, who combined art with social activism. This influence is evidenced in Alston's larger-than-life murals depicting Harlem Hospital. Alston was one of the first black supervisors for the Works Projects Administration and the first African American instructor at the Art Students League in New York; he also taught at City College from 1970 to 1977. His work is represented in the permanent collections of the Metropolitan Museum of Art and the Whitney Museum of American Art.

Carl Anderson (1945–2004)

Born in Lynchburg, Virginia, Anderson was one of 12 children. He became a well-known film star and prolific recording artist beginning in the 1970s; he was also an artist. In film, he appeared as Judas in *Jesus Christ Superstar* (1974) and subsequently in *The Black Pearl* (1978) and Steven Spielberg's *The Color Purple* (1985). On television he appeared in *Cop Rock*, *Days of our Lives*, and *Hill Street Blues*. As a recording artist, Anderson released nine jazz and soul albums. He collaborated with Stevie Wonder on the landmark double album *Songs in the Key of Life* (1976), and his influence can be heard in many recordings made in that decade. "Friends and Lovers," a duet with Gloria Loring, was the title song from a 1986 album. In 1992, he reprised the role of Judas on a national tour that lasted for five years and grossed over $100 million. A personal note: Anderson became a very close friend and traveling companion of the Kinseys. Sinalunga, Italy, a place they visited together, was the setting for his first painting.

Edward M. Bannister (1828–1901)

Bannister, born in Canada, was at a young age encouraged by his mother to paint. He moved to Boston in 1848 and became a barber, but pursued his love of art at the Lowell Institute, studying under sculptor William Rimmer. Influenced by the Barbizon School, Bannister painted idyllic landscapes with thick impasto. At the 1876 Centennial Exposition in Philadelphia, Bannister's *Under the Oaks* was selected for the bronze medal, the major prize for oil painting. He became a founding member of the Providence Art Club in 1880. He received many commissions and lived on proceeds from his work.

Ernie Barnes (1938–2009)

A former professional football player, Ernie Barnes is recognized as one of the foremost African American artists. Barnes was inspired to draw and paint beginning in early childhood. Awarded a football scholarship to attend the all-black North Carolina Central University, he went on to major in art. Following college, Barnes played professional football for five seasons. In 1965, New York Jets owner Sonny Werblin was responsible for Barnes' critically acclaimed debut at the Grand Central Art Galleries in New York. Barnes served as the "Official Sports Artist" for the 1984 Olympics in Los Angeles and was commissioned to paint *The Dream Unfolds* for the National Basketball Association in commemoration of its 50th anniversary. For over 40 years, his neo-mannerist style has been admired and collected internationally.

Richmond Barthé (1901–1989)

Barthé attended the Art Institute of Chicago. He studied painting with Charles Schroeder, who encouraged him to explore three-dimensional art,thus discovering a passion for sculpting. He was awarded two Rosenwald Fellowships, which enabled him to study at the Art Students League and in Paris, and he then received a Guggenheim Fellowship. In 1946, he was inducted into the National Institute of Arts and Letters. When artistic trends in America shifted toward abstractionism, Barthé left the country for a time, first residing in Jamaica, then in Italy. He moved to California in 1977. His sculptures have been collected by the Whitney Museum of American Art, the Metropolitan Museum of Art, and the Smithsonian, as well as many universities.

Romare Bearden (1911–1988)

Bearden's arts education began with Harlem Renaissance artists and scholars. He graduated from New York University, earning a degree in education. He also studied philosophy in Paris at the Sorbonne and art at the Art Students League in New York. Bearden, a social worker with the New York City Department of Social Services for over 25 years, translated this calling into social activism, which he carried out through both art and community involvement. In 1964, Bearden was appointed the first art director of the Harlem Cultural Council, which advocated for the African American community. He was a founding member of the Studio Museum in Harlem, and with fellow artists Norman Lewis and Ernest Crichlow created the Cinque Gallery to promote minority artists. He was a prolific writer, and his *History of African American Artists: From 1792 to the Present*, published posthumously, is a landmark in the scholarship on African American art. Bearden's work is represented in the Metropolitan Museum of Art, the Whitney Museum of American Art, the Philadelphia Museum of Art, the Museum of Fine Arts, Boston, and the Studio Museum in Harlem. He was elected to the National Institute of Arts and Letters in 1972, and in 1987 President Ronald Reagan awarded Bearden the National Medal of Arts.

Phoebe Beasley (1943–)

Beasley was born in Cleveland and earned a BFA from Ohio State University. After moving to Los Angeles, she sustained dual careers as an artist and a media executive. Beasley is the only artist to have earned a Presidential Seal on two occasions, for commissions from Presidents Clinton and George H. W. Bush. Beasley's work has been shown at the Kansas African American Museum and in a solo exhibition at the M. Hanks Gallery in Santa Monica, California. Another project was a collaboration with Maya Angelou, in which Beasley created several serigraphs based on poems by Langston Hughes for a limited edition book, *Sunrise is Coming after While*. Beasley's work has recently been featured in the touring exhibition "Portraying Lincoln: Man of Many Faces."

John Biggers (1924–2001)

Biggers attended Hampton Institute, where his talent was encouraged by Viktor Lowebfeld. In 1943, Biggers' mural *Dying Soldier* was featured in the exhibition "Young Negro Art" at the Museum of Modern Art in New York. Biggers was influenced by Harlem Renaissance thinkers and artists, including W. E. B. DuBois and Charles White, who became his mentor. Biggers enrolled at Pennsylvania State University and was awarded a doctorate in 1954. He was the founding chairman of the art department at Texas Southern University and initiated a mural program there. In 1957, Biggers received a UNESCO fellowship to study art in Africa, the basis of *Ananse: The Web of Life in Africa*, a visual diary of his experiences there.

Colin Bird (?–)

Australian Aboriginal artist, Colin Bird, is from Utopia, northeast of Alice Springs, in the Central Desert. He grew up working as a stockman and living off the land in a semi-traditional lifestyle. As the son of acclaimed Utopia woman artist Ada Bird Petyarre, and also inspired by his renowned artist uncle Lyndsay Bird Mpetyane, Bird began painting in the late eighties. He paints Ahakeye (bush plum), Ulkuta (perentie or lizard), ancestral snakes, and other motifs and stories, featuring meticulous patterning and bold color combinations. His paintings are owned by art collectors around the world.

Bob Blackburn (1920–2003)

Blackburn grew up in Harlem, where he attended art classes taught by Harlem Renaissance artists, and he studied lithography, etching, woodblock, and silk-screening at the Art Students League. In 1948, he began experimenting with innovative lithographic techniques. In the late '50s and early '60s, he worked as a master printer at Universal Limited Art Editions. With Will Barnet and Thomas Laidman, Blackburn founded and became the director of the Printmaking Workshop in New York. There he printed works with artists

Robert Rauschenberg, Charles White, and Eldzier Cortor, among others. Blackburn taught at Pratt Institute, Columbia University, and Rutgers University. In 1992, he received a John T. and Catherine D. MacArthur Foundation Fellowship, and in 2002, lifetime achievement awards from the College Art Association and the National Fine Print Association.

Grafton Tyler Brown (1841–1918)

Born in Harrisburg, Pennsylvania, Brown migrated to San Francisco in search of opportunities. He worked as a lithographer for C. C. Kuchel and in 1867 started his own company producing maps, plats, and bank notes for Wells Fargo, Levi Strauss Company, and other firms. In addition to lithography, Brown mastered classic landscape painting. His paintings of western landscapes are technically precise, yet they also reveal Brown's strong desire to document the threatened natural environment he loved. He sold his company to travel the West Coast, maintaining studios in Portland, Oregon, and then in British Columbia. In 1893, Brown moved east to St. Paul, Minnesota, to work as a draftsman for the U.S. Army Corps of Engineers. Much of his commercial work is a testament to both black craftsmanship and entrepreneurial spirit.

Margaret Burroughs (1917–)

Burroughs was born in St. Rose, Louisiana, in 1917, and moved with her family to the south side of Chicago in 1922. She graduated from Chicago Teachers College in 1937, studied at Chicago State, and became an art teacher at DuSable High School. She married fellow artist Bernard Goss in 1939, and their coach-house flat became a social center, dubbed "little Bohemia," for a wide and interracial circle of friends and colleagues. Burroughs worked tirelessly to establish the South Side Community

Art Center, which opened in 1940, and became the youngest member of its board. She later studied at the Art Institute of Chicago, receiving the MFA in 1948. Burroughs worked in many media, showing special facility in watercolors and linocut printmaking. An accomplished poet, she has also written children's books. In 1961, with Charles Burroughs, her second husband, she founded the DuSable Museum of African American History in Chicago, which stands as one of the premier institutions for documenting and displaying the African American experience.

Bisa Butler (1975–)

Butler, born in Orange, New Jersey, graduated from Howard University, where she studied the work of Howard professors and students, including Lois Mailou Jones and Elizabeth Catlett. While working on her MFA, Butler began to merge her love of fabric with artistic expression, creating vibrant quilts that depict black life. She notes, "With fiber art, I feel that I have finally tapped into a way to communicate emotion, art, heritage, tradition, and beauty to those who view my work." Recently, a Butler quilt of voters in line at the polls was featured in a special exhibition at the Washington Historical Society in honor of then President-elect Barack Obama.

William Sylvester Carter (1909-1996)

Carter, a nationally recognized and award-winning artist, lived on Chicago's south side for most of his life and contributed extensively to the African American art culture of the city. Carter mastered all painting mediums to convey a poignant visual journal of a people confined within the American closet. Most of all, Carter leads the viewer to a profound appreciation of the irony and complexity of their experience, balanced by admiration for their

cohesive urban spirit and the vibrant hope that tomorrow will be brighter.

Elizabeth Catlett (1915–)

Catlett, one of the most famous and prolific women sculptors of the 20th century, was the first African American to earn an MFA from the University of Iowa. In 1940, her thesis project, a limestone sculpture entitled *Mother and Child*, won first prize in sculpture at the Negro Exposition in Chicago. She studied ceramics at the Chicago Institute of Art and lithography at the Art Students League. She received a Rosenwald Fellowship to study wood and ceramic sculpture in Mexico, where she befriended many muralists and worked with the People's Graphic Arts Workshop. She married artist Francisco Mora and became a Mexican citizen. Her work is included in the permanent collections of Museum of Modern Art and the Metropolitan Museum of Art in New York, as well as the National Institute of Fine Arts in Mexico City and the National Museum in Prague.

Michael Chukes (1961–)

Born in Vallejo, Chukes began creating artworks at a very young age, then earned a BFA from California College of Arts and Crafts in Oakland, and a MFA from Claremont Graduate University. Chukes' human form surreal sculptures are made of clay, bronze, wood, and other materials, and include exaggerated body parts and his own color technique. He "concentrates on capturing emotional sensations of the body rather than its physical presence". Chukes' work has been on display at numerous museums and galleries, and he lectures and facilitates workshops around the country.

Claude Clark (1915–2001)

Clark attended the Pennsylvania School of

Industrial Arts, and from 1939 to 1942 worked as a Works Projects Administration artist in its graphic arts division. He furthered his study of art at the Barnes Foundation in Merion, Pennsylvania, and taught art at Talladega College in Alabama. He earned bachelor's and master's degrees at Sacramento State College and the University of California, Berkeley, respectively. Clark continued to dedicate himself to the education of others, teaching at Merritt College until his retirement in 1981. He also designed the first curriculum for African and African American Art.

Eldzier Cortor (1916–)

Cortor grew up on the south side of Chicago and in 1935 attended drawing classes at the Art Institute. In 1940, he worked for the Works Projects Administration in Chicago with Charles Sebree, Charles White, and Bernard Goss. In the 1940s, he studied woodblock techniques at Columbia University. He was very interested in African art and explored the residual cultural elements of African origins in Georgia's Sea Islands. He was awarded a Rosenwald Fellowship and later, a Guggenheim, which underwrote his study of African artistic and cultural influences in Haiti, Cuba, and Jamaica. African American women are the thematic focus of Cortor's work because he believed the black woman is the essential spirit of the race, conveying "a feeling of eternity and continuance of life." Although Cortor is best known for his early work, in the 1970s his art enjoyed resurgent interest, shown in major exhibitions at the Boston Museum of Fine Arts, the Studio Museum of Harlem, and the National Center of Afro-American Artists in Boston.

Allan Rohan Crite (1910–2007)

Crite's mother, Annamae, was a poet who en-

couraged her son to draw. He studied at the school of the Museum of Fine Arts in Boston and later attended Harvard University Extension. His drawings and paintings depict religious themes, African American daily life, and street scenes of his Boston neighborhood. In 1936, his work was exhibited at the Museum of Modern Art in New York and at Harvard University's Fogg Museum. Other galleries and museums that featured major exhibitions of his work include the Harmon Foundation and the Corcoran Gallery of Art. Crite's work can be found in the permanent collections of the Boston Museum of Fine Arts, the Boston Public Library, the Library of the Boston Athenaeum, the Museum of the National Center of Afro-American Artists, the Phillips Collection, the Smithsonian Institution, and the Art Institute of Chicago.

Bill Dallas (1937–)

Dallas received a BFA in painting from the University of California, Berkeley. His travels have taken him to nearly twenty different countries, where he has studied art and other varieties of cultural expression. In Japan he studied with master artist Toshi Yoshida. Dallas' work, distinguished for its exploration of the rhythm and tempo of music, has been exhibited throughout the San Francisco and New York areas and is held in private collections in Australia, Brazil, Denmark, Germany, Japan, New Zealand, and South Africa, as well as the United States.

Alonzo Davis (1942–)

Born in Tuskagee, Alabama, Alonzo Davis earned his MFA from Otis Art Institute in Los Angeles. In his many series of woven paintings and prints, Davis uses paint, bamboo, copper, leather, quilts, indigenous textiles and mixed media to reflect the magic of the Southwest United States, Brazil, Haiti, West Africa and

the Pacific Rim. Inspired by travel, he seeks "influences, cultural centers, energies, new terrain and the power of both the spoken and unspoken". Davis lives in Southern California.

Beauford Delaney (1901–1978)

Delaney's exodus from the South was sponsored by his Knoxville mentor Lloyd Branson. He furthered his education in Boston before moving to New York, where he worked odd jobs and maintained a studio in Greenwich Village. He befriended Harlem artists, but his anxiety over his homosexuality kept him isolated from much of Harlem life. Delaney loved music, and his figurative and abstract work is fluid and expressive, resembling a visible jazz. In 1949, he joined his friend James Baldwin in Paris. His efforts in abstract expressionism flourished, and his work enjoyed a brief resurgence of interest in the period before his death. In 1978, the Studio Museum of Harlem mounted a major retrospective of his Paris work.

Aaron Douglas (1899–1979)

Douglas, born in Topeka, Kansas, earned a bachelor's degree from the University of Nebraska. He came to New York in the 1920s and studied under German artist Winold Reiss. Douglas infused his drawings and paintings with elements of traditional African styles and design. His illustrations appeared in national magazines, the written work of Alain Locke and James Weldon Johnson, as well as in DuBois' periodical *The Crisis*. In 1928, he became the Harlem Artist Guild's first president, and he was instrumental in securing WPA projects for black artists. He founded the art department at Fisk University in 1939, where he worked until his retirement in the late 1960s.

Robert Scott Duncanson (1817–1872)

Duncanson, born in Seneca, New York, spent

his early years in Canada with his Scottish father. He later moved to Ohio to live with his black mother, where he pursued his love of painting. He began his professional life as a portrait painter but was drawn to landscape, and his work was greatly influenced by the Hudson River School. He was commissioned to do several large murals in Cincinnati, and these were well received, enabling him to live off the proceeds of his work. Later, he traveled to Britain to study and paint landscapes. The *London Art Journal* declared him a master painter. After his death, however, his work fell into obscurity. It was not until the 1950s, when James Porter dedicated himself to reclaiming Duncanson's contribution to African American art, that his work was rediscovered by the public.

Samuel L. Dunson, Jr. (1970–)

Dunson showed a talent for art as a youth. He attended Tennessee State University, where he began to paint in earnest. He earned his bachelor's degree in 1992 and continued his education at the Savannah College of Art and Design, earning an MFA in 2000. He returned to Tennessee State as an assistant professor. He continues to paint, and to exhibit his work throughout the United States.

Ed Dwight (1933–)

Dwight's first major commission was to create a sculpture of George Brown, Colorado's first black Lt. Governor. For the Colorado Centennial Commission, Dwight was asked to produce 30 bronzes depicting the contributions of African Americans to the expansion of the West. In the series "Jazz: An American Art Form," Dwight explored the musical contributions of jazz to the fabric of American life and culture. Dwight has been involved with many public art projects, including monuments in Detroit and in Windsor, Canada, dedicated to the Underground Railroad. His largest memorial work, honoring Martin Luther King, Jr., is installed in Denver. His autobiography, *Soaring on the Wings of a Dream*, was recently published by Third World Press.

Sam Gilliam (1933–)

Born in Tupelo, Mississippi, Gilliam received his formal art education at the University of Louisville. He moved to Washington, D.C., and established a connection with prominent color-field artists. In 1967 he received a National Endowment for the Arts grant. Gilliam is best known for his draped cloth paintings, using both color and gravity to shape the freed canvas. He has produced a number of outdoor sculptures, including an installation at Philadelphia Museum of Art in 1975 and another at the California African American Museum in Los Angeles. In the 1970s, he experimented with white paintings, covering richly textured color-field work with impasto and glaze. In his later work, he has turned to solidly three-dimensional structures made of wood and mixed media. In 2005, the Corcoran Gallery of Art in Washington, D.C., held a major retrospective of Gilliam's work.

Jonathan Green (1955–)

Green earned his bachelor of fine arts degree from the Art Institute of Chicago in 1982. The scenes he depicts in his work focus on themes of work, love, belonging, and spirituality in the African American experience, and are heavily influenced by his childhood immersion in the Gullah culture of South Carolina. *Gullah Images: The Art of Jonathan Green* was published by University of South Carolina Press in 1996. Green's work has been exhibited in major museums and is held in many private and public collections, including the Philharmonic Center for the Arts in Naples, Florida; the Morris Museum of Art in Augusta, Georgia; the Norton Museum of Art in West Palm Beach, Florida; the Gibbes Museum of Art in Charleston, South Carolina; and the McKissick Museum of the University of South Carolina, in Columbia.

Robert Gwathmey (1903–1988)

Born in Richmond, Virginia, Gwathmey grew up experiencing the harsh realities of social stratification. He worked to help support his family and discovered his passion for art while he worked on a freighter in Europe. There, he began to visit museums and formulate a perspective that he would explore further during a year at Baltimore's Maryland Institute of Design. He earned a degree from the Pennsylvania Academy of the Fine Arts, where he studied from 1926 to 1930. He developed a cubist style of representation that would earn him acclaim in the 1940s. Like many of his African American peers, he was an inspiring teacher, and he served on the faculty of Cooper Union as a drawing instructor until 1968. Gwathmey was elected to the American Academy and Institute of Arts and Letters, and in 1976 became an associate member of the National Academy of Design.

John Wesley Hardwick (1891–1968)

Hardwick first exhibited his art at the Negro Business League convention and the Indiana State Fair in 1904 when he was only 13 years old. Later he attended Herron School of Art in Indianapolis and studied with William Forsyth. In the early 1920s, Hardwick shared a studio with Hale Woodruff, and their work was exhibited together at the Art Institute of Chicago. In 1927, Hardwick received a bronze award from the Harmon Foundation for his painting *Portrait of a Young Girl*. He continued to receive support from the Harmon Foundation for five more years, and his work was exhibited in museums around the country, including the Indianapolis Museum of Art and the Smithsonian. In 1934, Hardwick was awarded a Works Projects Administration commission to paint a mural for Crispus Attucks High School in Indianapolis. The mural, *Workers*, portrayed three African American foundry workers pouring molten metal; it was never mounted, however.

Palmer Hayden (1890–1973)

Born Peyton Cole Hedgeman in Wide Water, Virginia, Hayden served in the military from 1914 to 1919. In 1925, he began studying with Asa G. Randall at the art colony in Boothbay, Maine. He won a Harmon Foundation Gold Award in 1926 for a Maine seascape. In Paris subsequently, he experimented with African motifs and black American subjects in his work. He then returned to New York, and in 1933 *Fetiche et Fleurs*, a work produced in Paris, was shown in the Exhibition of the Works of Negro Artists at the Harmon Foundation, and won the Mrs. John D. Rockefeller Prize. Hayden worked for the WPA from 1934 to 1938, producing a series of paintings depicting the legendary John Henry. Many of his works shed light on the experiences of African Americans in the rural South, including *Hog Killing Time in Virginia*. In 1973, Hayden was commissioned to paint a series on black American soldiers through a fellowship from the Creative Artist Public Service Program of New York, but he died before he could begin work on it.

Kennith Humphrey (1965-)

Humphrey, an internationally recognized artist, currently resides in Vicksburg, Mississippi, the town of his birth, though in his thirties he ranged widely, working as a carpenter, shingler, electronic technician, tower climber, and landscaper in New York, Denver, St. Louis, Mobile, and Baton Rouge. His journey as an artist began at home in Vicksburg, where a

painting by an uncle that hung in his childhood home made the idea of being an artist seem realistic and attainable. He found a mentor in his half-brother, the late William Tolliver, a successful artist. Most of Humphrey's oils on canvas and pastel/acrylics on paper are stylized, sometimes cubist, depictions of African-American figures involved in the activities of daily life. Yet Humphrey's strongly emotional works cannot be classified in a single style. His free-flowing painted sketches, marked by elements of Impressionism, continue to speak of struggle and triumph.

Richard Hunt (1935–)

Hunt developed his skills at the Junior School of the Art Institute and later at the University of Illinois, Chicago. Early in his career, he experimented with various materials and sculpting techniques but is best known for his works in bronze and stainless steel. He was the youngest artist represented in the survey of modern art exhibition that was presented at the 1962 Seattle World's Fair. Hunt's best-known works include *Jacob's Ladder*, now at the Carter G. Woodson Library in Chicago, and *Flintlock Fantasy*, now in Detroit. President Lyndon Johnson appointed him to serve on the governing board of the National Endowment for the Arts; he was the first artist to hold this position. Hunt's work is included in the permanent collection of the Museum of Modern Art.

Kwesi Hutchful (1979–)

Hutchful is a Ghanaian and Canadian photographer and film-maker who now resides in the Lake Merritt area of Oakland, California. He developed a deep interest in photography in 1996, and he began to blend it with his love for anthropology. The complex style of his work goes beyond formalism, extending the context of the image and engaging the viewer as both

an observer and a participant. His photographs, through the use of detail and light, embrace the eye and lead the mind on a surprising journey. His work has often been described as elegant yet mysterious, and hauntingly beautiful.

May Howard Jackson (1877–1931)

Jackson was born and educated in Philadelphia. In 1895, she became the first African American woman to be accepted to the Pennsylvania Academy of the Fine Arts, where she studied with William Merritt Chase and John Joseph Boyle. African Americans, particularly those of mixed ancestry, are the focus of her sculptures. Jackson created portrait busts of Paul Lawrence Dunbar and W. E. B. Dubois, among others. She also painted abstract portraits, such as *Head of Negro Child* and *Mulatto Mother and Child*. She declined invitations to study in Paris, and while her work reflects the expressive style of the times, her perspective as a black woman is evident. Jackson joined the art department at Howard University in 1922. Her work was exhibited at the Corcoran Gallery in Washington, D.C., in 1915, and at the National Academy of Design in 1916 and 1928.

Buena Johnson (1954 –)

Johnson received her BFA in Communications Design from the Pratt Institute of Art in New York. She is a trained illustrator, teacher, photographer and fine artist. Inspired by the intricate line drawings of German Renaissance artist Albrecht Durer, Johnson draws with a photographic realism style that captures minute detail to intensify reality. Using symbolic imagery, her aim is "to present a message that will uplift, encourage and inspire the spirit of the viewer". Johnson worked for several years in advertising and editorial work for major corporations, book publishers, magazines, and newspapers. She has lectured, done art demonstrations, and exhibited throughout the United States and Japan, and currently resides in Southern California. Her painting on page 121 was commission by the Torrance Chamber of Commerce as a gift to Mr. Kinsey for his outstanding community service in 2004.

William H. Johnson (1901–1970)
Born in Florence, South Carolina, Johnson moved to New York City when he was 17 to pursue a career as an artist. At 20, he enrolled at the National Academy of Design, where he was mentored by Charles Hawthorne. In 1926, Johnson moved to Paris, where he met artists Henry Tanner and Palmer Hayden and Danish artist Holche Krake, whom he would later marry. Johnson returned to New York in 1929 and won the Harmon Foundation Gold Award. He turned his attention toward a more primitive style of painting that employed bold colors and block figures. A large number of his paintings were gathered by the Harmon Foundation and given to the National Museum of American Art in Washington, D.C.

Lois Mailou Jones (1905–1998)
Jones studied art at Boston High School of Practical Arts, the Boston Museum School of Fine Arts, and the Designers Art School of Boston. She earned her bachelor's degree from Howard University in 1945, graduating magna cum laude. She joined the faculty at Howard, serving as professor of design and watercolor painting until her retirement in 1977. In the 1930s, Jones took a sabbatical and traveled to Paris to study. She designed African-style masks and painted *Les Fétiches* as well as portraits of friends and artists she met in Paris. Jones' ongoing stylistic experimentation with African themes, expressionism, and depictions of her beloved Martha's Vineyard created a

vast oeuvre. She married Haitian artist Louis Vergniaud Pierre-Noel in 1953, and for a time lived in Haiti. Jones received an honorary doctorate of Humane Letters from Suffolk University in Boston, and was elected Fellow of the Royal Society of Arts in London. In 1980, President Jimmy Carter honored her achievements at the White House.

Artis Lane (1927–)
A descendent of renowned abolitionist Mary Ann Shadd, Lane was awarded a scholarship to the Ontario College of Art in Toronto and was the first woman admitted to Cranbrook Art Academy. Her early career as a portrait painter began with Michigan Governor George Romney as her subject. Lane continued her portraiture in Los Angeles, depicting dignitaries Nelson Mandela, Gordon Getty, Ronald Reagan, Barbara Bush, and others. She used artistic expression to address social and spiritual issues with such works as *The Beginning*, depicting a young Rosa Parks seated on the bus. She was to become Parks' personal portrait artist. Lane eventually shifted her focus to sculpture, creating lithe dancers, pregnant women, and her generic man/woman series. Lane's latest series, *Emerging into Spirit*, includes fragmented pieces of ceramic shell left on her bronzes that symbolize man's spiritual journey to enlightenment.

Jacob Lawrence (1917–2000)
Schooled by Charles Alston and other Harlem Renaissance notables, Lawrence received his early education in Harlem. Growing up, he observed the daily life of African Americans, and these scenes comprise much of Lawrence's subject matter. In 1937, at the age of 21, Lawrence created 41 paintings documenting the rise and fall of Toussant L'Ouverture, Haiti's revolutionary leader. His series on the Great Migration, which combines stylistic interpreta-

tion with a historically grounded perspective on black life, was acquired by the Metropolitan Museum of Art in New York, making Lawrence the first African American artist represented in that institution's permanent collection. He served on the faculty at the Art Students League, the Skowhegan School in Maine, and Pratt Institute, and in 1970, moved to Seattle with his wife, painter Gwendolyn Knight, to take up an appointment as a professor in the School of Art at the University of Washington. He retired in 1980. Lawrence's work earned him a National Medal of Arts as well as election to the National Academy of Arts and Letters and the National Academy of Design.

Hughie Lee-Smith (1915–1999)
Lee-Smith, born in Eustis, Florida, attended the Cleveland Institute of Art and later earned an arts education degree from Wayne State University. In 1940, his work was exhibited at the American Negro Exposition in Chicago. Lee-Smith painted murals during his service in the Navy, and for the Works Projects Administration in Ohio and Illinois. The pointed social commentary expressed in his work limited its appeal to a wide audience, and his figurative paintings of isolated youth did not conform to the abstract expressionism dominant at the time, yet he enjoyed a position of respect within the African American arts community. In 1994, he was commissioned to paint New York Mayor David Dinkins' portrait. Lee-Smith's work has been shown in the Whitney Museum of American Art and the Museum of Modern Art. In 1988, the New Jersey State Museum mounted a retrospective of his work.

Norman Lewis (1909–1979)
Born in Harlem, Lewis studied art in the 1930s with Augusta Savage and later with Raphael Soyer at the John Reed Art School. He

graduated from Columbia University but subsequently rejected formal study and began to work for the Works Projects Administration. The figurative paintings characteristic of Lewis' early work are forceful and emotional; his later works were increasingly abstract. He was active in the Artist Union and the Harlem Artist Guild and he was a founding member of the Spiral Group. In 1955, *Migrating Birds* won the Popular Prize at the Carnegie International Exhibition. In 1970, he became a member of the American Academy of Arts and Letters, and in 1971 the National Institute of Arts and Letters; during the '70s, when he was an instructor at the Art Students League, his work earned wider recognition. He was the recipient of grants from the Mark Rothko Foundation, the National Endowment for the Arts, and the Guggenheim Foundation.

Samella Lewis (1924–)

Born in New Orleans, Lewis began drawing and painting at age 4, studied art at Dillard University under Elizabeth Catlett, received a BA in art from Hampton University, and a MA and PhD in Fine Arts and Art History from Ohio State University. Lewis was the chair of the Fine Arts Department of Florida A&M University, earned a Fulbright Fellowship to study Asian art in Taiwan, and was a professor at State College of New York and the Scripps College in Claremont, CA. She was the education coordinator at the Los Angeles County Museum of Art, and founded the Museum of African American Art in Los Angeles and the scholarly journal, the *International Review of African American Art*. She produced films on individual artists and a general history film *The Black Artist*. She edited, wrote, and published books including the textbook *Art: African American*. Her deeply personal works of art, in a variety of media, were based upon her own childhood, the experiences of African Americans in the South, and her exploration of the artistic cultures of African diaspora.

Lionel Lofton (1954–)

Lofton, best known as a printmaker, also works frequently in acrylic, watercolor, pencil, and collage. A native of Houston, Lofton has been interested in art since childhood and has pursued formal studies at Texas Southern University, Prairie View A&M, and University of Houston, Clear Lake. Lofton's works, which have been shown in important galleries and exhibits throughout the U.S., have a quietly introspective air that conveys the character of their creator. His art powerfully expresses the spirituality and beauty of everyday experience, as he says, "Art is a part of living."

Ed Loper (1916–)

At 20 years of age, Loper began working for the Index of American Design of the Works Progress Administration. Albert Barnes invited him to take classes at the Barnes Foundation in Merion, Pennsylvania, and he subsequently became a full-time artist and art teacher. His technique of "fractured realism" closely resembles figurative abstraction; his boldly colored images look as if refracted through a prism. Loper recently donated his personal papers to the Historical Society of Delaware's Research Library. His paintings can be found in many private collections and in the permanent collections of the Delaware Art Museum, the Philadelphia Museum of Art, the Corcoran Gallery of Art, the Museum of American Art at the Pennsylvania Academy of Fine Arts, and Howard University Gallery of Art.

Ricardo Losada (?–)

Authors' Note: We are unable to provide any biographical information on this Cuban artist. On a 2003 trip to Havanna with Congresswoman Barbara Lee, we fell for, but did not immediately acquire, a Losada painting in a gallery at Hotel Nacionel. On our last day, our audience with Premier Fidel Castro was an awesome experience that extended on close to our airplane departure time. The Premier said "don't worry, the plane will wait", and wait it did... We rushed back to the hotel for our luggage, purchased the Losada painting, and made it home, with fond memories of the Cuban people.

Richard Mayhew (1924–)

Mayhew, born in Amityville, New York, studied at the Art Students League and Hans Hofmann's School of Fine Art in New York. Under Hofman, Mayhew pursued abstract expressionism and joined it to his spiritual appreciation of nature to create improvisational landscapes. Mayhew also earned an art history degree from Columbia University. After his tour of duty during World War II, he worked as a singer and pursued a career as a medical illustrator. In 1951, he began his studies at the Brooklyn Museum of Art and in 1955 had a solo exhibition there. After studying at the MacDowell Colony in New Hampshire in 1958, he was awarded a John Hay Whitney fellowship, which allowed him to study at the Accademia in Florence, Italy. He returned to New York and with a group of African American artists formed the Spiral Group, founded to address political issues and later drawn to aesthetic ones, seeking to define what Ralph Ellison called "a new visual order." His work is in the permanent collections of the Smithsonian, the Whitney Museum of American Art, and the Brooklyn Museum of Art.

Kadir Nelson (1974-   )

Nelson began drawing at the age of three, and painting at age ten. Under the encouragement and tutelage of both his uncle and high school art teacher, Nelson experimented with several different media and began painting in oils at sixteen, won several competitions, and was awarded a scholarship to the Pratt Institute in New York. An honors graduate, he immediately began publishing his work and receiving commissions. He served as a lead conceptual artist for Steven Spielberg's *Amistad* and *Spirit: Stallion of the Cimarron*. Among his clients are Sports Illustrated, Coca-Cola, the United States Postal Service, and Major League Baseball. His work has been exhibited in galleries and museums in Mexico, England, and Japan as well as major American venues. In 1999, Nelson began to illustrate children's picture books, and he has been honored with a Coretta Scott King Illustrator Award, a Caldecott Medal, and an NAACP Image Award. Nelson's strongly emotional style is instantly recognizable, despite the variety of subjects he has treated. As he has put it, "My focus is to create images of people who demonstrate a sense of hope and nobility. I want to show the strength and integrity of the human being and the human spirit."

William Pajaud (1925–   )

Palaud studied at Xavier University in New Orleans, earning a BFA degree. He arrived in Los Angeles in 1948 and attended Chouinard Art Institute, the first African American to be admitted and to complete the program. In 1957, he became the art director and artist for Golden State Mutual Insurance Company, an African–American owned company based in Los Angeles. Later, he curated the company's art collection, which became one of the most famous collections of African American art in the U.S. Pajaud continued to create work during his tenure at Golden State. Black women are often featured in his work, as he admires their beauty and their strength, and their perseverance from slavery forward. His paintings, in both oil and watercolor, are figurative. His work can be found in the permanent collections of the Amistad Research Center in New Orleans, the Las Vegas Museum of Art, the California African American Museum, the Norton Simon Museum in Los Angeles, and the Smithsonian American Art Museum in Washington, D.C.

Gordon Parks (1912–2006)

Parks was named after a Dr. Gordon, who had saved his life at birth. Parks is internationally renowned as a photographer, film-maker, novelist, and composer. In 1947, he became the first black photographer at *Life* magazine. Parks' documentary style produced provocative images, including *American Gothic*, Washington, D.C., his riveting commentary on racism in America. He documented the civil rights movement in the 1950s and 1960s, to national acclaim. His autobiographical novel *The Learning Tree* led to his directorial debut in feature films. He continued to produce documentary and fine art photography.

Charles Ethan Porter (ca. 1847–1923)

Porter's style skillfully merged Barbizon influences into an American perspective, and represents the best of American artistry in landscape, still life, and portraiture. He was one of the first black artists to study and exhibit at New York's National Academy of Design. Porter traveled to Paris and was introduced to art circles through a letter of recommendation from Mark Twain. In France, he studied at L'Ecole des Arts Decoratifs and spent time studying landscapes near Barbizon. He returned to the U.S. and settled in Connecticut, where he continued to paint. In 1910, Porter became a charter member of the Connecticut Academy of Fine Arts.

James Porter (1905–1970)

James Porter attended Howard University and later joined its art department, where he taught painting and drawing. In 1933, he received the Schomburg Portrait Prize from the Harmon Foundation for *Woman Holding a Jug*. In 1943, he published *Modern Negro Art*, which sought to acknowledge the achievement of African American artists and to place their work in a broader art context. Porter focused his academic research on black artists who were not recognized by the mainstream, including 19th-century painter Robert S. Duncanson, whom he rescued from obscurity. In 1945, he received a Rockefeller Foundation grant that allowed him to study Cuban and Haitian art. Porter chaired the art department at Howard University and served as the director of the Howard University Gallery of Art from 1953 to 1970.

Edward Pratt (1957–   )

Edward Pratt, an educator and painter, grew up in Washington D.C. He studied with sculptor and painter Phillip Ratner and went on to the Hampton Institute in Virginia and studied in France. Pratt worked for the prestigious Barnett-Aden Collection in Washington, D.C. In 1989, one of his paintings was featured on the cover of *Art Now* magazine. His work is held in many corporate and private collections in the United States and in Europe.

Toni Scott (1959–   )

Scott, a native Californian, trained at Otis College of Art and Design, earned a BA from the University of Southern California, and has studied privately with artists Joan Carl,

Charles Dickson, Richard Ellis, and John Paul Thornton. Scott is a versatile multi-media artist working in sculpture, painting, photography, and digital design. An interracial woman of African, European, and Native American heritage, she finds inspiration in the richness of her history and four generations of artists and musicians. Award-winning and exhibited and collected worldwide, Scott's diverse and distinctive artwork always expresses her love of God, beauty, humanity and culture.

Maxon Scylla (?–)

Maxon Scylla creates sequined banners, "Drapo Vodou", an art form unique to Haiti. Scylla's brother-in-law, famous Haitian artist Antoine Oleyant, brought Haitian ceremonial flags out of the Vodou Temple and into the realm of fine art. When Oleyant decided to devote full-time to his art, he opened his workshop with brother-in-law flag-maker Scylla. After Oleyant's death in 1992, Scylla has continued the art with his own uniquely beautiful color palette perfecting Oleyant's drawings.

Henry O. Tanner (1859–1925)

Tanner, born in Pittsburgh, was the first African American to attend the Pennsylvania Academy of the Fine Arts, where he studied with and became a favorite student of Thomas Eakins. The lack of opportunities in Philadelphia due to racial discrimination contributed to Tanner's decision to leave the United States for Paris in 1891. With the help of renowned artist Jean Paul Lauren and others, Tanner gained considerable recognition for his religious paintings. *The Resurrection of Lazarus* in particular earned him a travel grant from art critic Rodman Wannamaker, and he went to the Middle East to further his study of religious art. Tanner's work continued to garner international praise; W. E. B. DuBois and oth-

ers tried to persuade him to return to the United States, to lead the black aesthetic movement, but Tanner remained in Europe and became host to many African American artists. *The Banjo Lesson* remains his most widely known work. *Sand Dunes at Sunset, Atlantic City* was the first work by an African American artist to be included in the White House permanent collection.

Terciliano, Jr. (1939–)

Terciliano, Jr., of Afro-Brazilian heritage, creates large abstract paintings devoted to the ritual arts of the African diasporic religion Candomblé. He paints the "ineffable qualities of the gods and their spiritual essence, or ase." He explains, "I try to do work that is truly representative of Black people, not caricatures of Black culture." Terciliano's work has evolved in major stylistic ways, but always "celebrates his family, his ancestors, and the generations of Afro-Brazilians who have kept the gods of Africa alive and well in the hearts and minds of Brazilians today".

Alma Thomas (1891–1978)

Alma Thomas was the first graduate of the Howard University art department, and the first black woman to earn an MFA from Columbia University. After teaching in the Washington, D.C., public schools for 35 years, she began her professional career in earnest. She was among the color-field painters active in Washington and shared a collaborative relationship with friends Morris Louis, Kenneth Nolan and Gene Davis. In 1943, she was asked by James Vernon Herring and Alonzo Aden to join them in establishing the Barnett-Aden Gallery, the first African American gallery in Washington. In 1971, when she was 80 years old, she was the first female African American artist to be recognized in a solo exhibition at

the Whitney Museum of American Art.

Matthew Thomas (1943–)

Thomas, born in San Antonio, Texas, came to Los Angeles with his family when he was a boy, and was exposed early to the ethnic and cultural melting pot of Southern California. In 1967, he graduated from the Chouinard School of Fine Arts. Thomas, a lay Buddhist monk who travels the world, has extended his exploration of Buddhism into his artistic practice. He uses a dynamic and brilliant range of colors, and his oeuvre conveys serenity and symmetry. He combines themes of science and religion in his work, seeking to reveal the intersections of our physical and spiritual universes. These connections are also evident in his work as ways to exchange ideas and seek wisdom through faith and artistic expression.

Dox Thrash (1892–1965)

Thrash, born in Georgia, left at age 15 in the Great Migration to find work in Chicago. He worked as a janitor by day and attended classes at the Art Institute at night. In 1917, he joined the army and was assigned to the 365th Infantry Regiment, 183rd Brigade, 92nd Division, famously known as the "Buffalo Soldiers." After the war, he returned to Chicago but traveled extensively, finally settling in Philadelphia, where he worked for the Federal Art Project from 1936 to 1939. Working with artists Michael Gallagher and Hubert Mesibov, Thrash invented the process of carborundum mezzotint, a revolutionary technique that employed carborundum instead of tools or other materials to etch copper plates. The grainy finish allowed Thrash to create provocative images, which he employed to depict scenes of African American life. Thrash made this process his primary medium and through it produced his greatest works.

In 2002, the Philadelphia Museum of Art mounted a major retrospective exhibit featuring over one hundred of his drawings, watercolors, and prints.

Dane Tilghman (?–)

Tilghman, a native Pennsylvanian, earned his BFA from Kutztown University, PA. His art has evolved from realism to his own interpretation of surrealism, impressionism, and primitive elongation. His images are inspired by African Americans in daily life, popular entertainment, and the world of sports. Tilghman is a premier painter of American Golf Art and Negro League Baseball images. His work has been widely exhibited since 1979. In 1999, a Tilghman baseball image was incorporated into the Baseball Hall of Fame Museum in Cooperstown. He has painted numerous commissioned murals at sports stadiums, and his art is included in many art products. "I emphasize Black Americana, but my work crosses over to a broad audience," says Tilghman. "I think everyone can relate to the old times and traditions and that all people can connect with the work."

William Tolliver (1951–2000)

Primarily self-taught as an artist, Tolliver, who was born in Mississippi, received some formal training from apprenticeships during his work with the Los Angeles Job Corps and in Wisconsin, where he assisted a local sculptor. Later, he married and moved to Lafayette, Louisiana, where he worked in the oil industry and painted whenever he wasn't working. His wife took his paintings to Bob Crutchfield, owner of Lafayette's Live Oak Gallery, where his work sold out, and Crutchfield asked for more. Tolliver believed that art was a means for documenting one's history, and he used the technique of figurative abstraction to depict scenes of rural black life in the South. His paintings have been exhibited at the Contemporary Art Center of New Orleans, the New Orleans Museum of Art, and the Senate office building in Washington, D.C.

Laura Wheeler Waring (1887–1948)

Wheeler, born in Hartford, Connecticut, began her formal arts education at the Pennsylvania Academy of the Fine Arts in 1908. After graduation, she founded the art department of the State Normal School at Cheyney, Pennsylvania, teaching and painting for over thirty years. She married Walter Waring, a professor at Lincoln University in Philadelphia. She earned acclaim as a portrait artist, and produced still life and landscapes as well. Her work was displayed in major museums, including the Art Institute of Chicago and the Smithsonian. In 1943, the Harmon Foundation commissioned her to paint a series of portraits of outstanding black citizens, including W. E. B. Dubois, Marion Anderson, and James Weldon Johnson.

Keith Morris Washington (1956 –)

Born in Gary, Indiana, Washington earned a BFA from Massachusetts College of Art and an MFA from Tufts University/School of the Museum of Fine Art, in Boston. His natural progression of artistic exploration took him "from realism, to geometric abstraction, to self-discovery via semi-abstract African iconography, back to my (his) first love, landscapes". Influenced by 19th century Hudson River, Barbizon and Luminist painting, Washington has developed several on going "dramatically thematic series of landscape paintings…the most logical mode to express my commitments to peace, justice, and my identity as both American.. and all that implies, and as an African American with all those ramifications…" Washington lives in Boston and is on the faculty of Massachusetts College of Art.

James Lesesne Wells (1902–1993)

Wells earned bachelor's and master's degrees from Columbia University, and studied at the National Academy of Design under George Laurence Nelson. In 1929, he joined the faculty at Howard University as a crafts teacher, where he created the graphics art department. His innovative approach to lithography and woodcut printmaking was driven by his desire to facilitate appreciation of the arts by ordinary people. His work often focused on religious themes, reflecting his upbringing as the son of a Baptist minister, and he was often inspired by African and cubist design. In 1931, Wells won the Harmon Foundation Gold Award for *Flight into Egypt*, and two years later he was awarded the foundation's George E. Haynes prize for the best black-and-white woodcut. In 1980, Wells was honored by President Jimmy Carter for achievements throughout his life.

Charles White (1918–1979)

White, born in Chicago, began his career at the Chicago Community Arts Center before receiving a full scholarship to the school of the Art Institute. In 1939, he worked as a mural painter for the Illinois Federal Arts Project, and later studied at the Art Students League in New York. White made prints at the renowned graphics workshop Taller de Grafica in Mexico City, where he lived for two years. After serving as artist in residence at Howard University, he moved to New York and worked with the Graphic Workshop. He said of his art, "I am a Negro in America. I relate to images that are meaningful to me, images that are closest to me. I use that as a springboard to deal with the more broad and the more all-encompassing." White was awarded two

Rosenwald fellowships, and in 1972 was elected a member of the National Academy of Design. He taught at the Otis Art Institute in Los Angeles from 1965 until his death.

Ernest Withers (1922–1987)

Withers was a prominent documentary photographer. Although he is best known for images of Dr. Martin Luther King, Jr., and the civil rights movement, from the bus boycott in Montgomery, Alabama, to the assassination of Dr. King in Memphis, his subject matter included early performances of entertainers (Elvis Presley, B.B. King, Ray Charles, Aretha Franklin), baseball players of the Diamond League (Willie Mays and Jackie Robinson), and the blues and jazz scene in Memphis, his hometown. He was awarded "Best Photographer of the Year" in 1968 by the National News Association, and his photographs appeared in *Time, Newsweek, Ebony, Jet*, the *New York Times, Washington Post*, the *Chicago Defender*, and the PBS documentary "Eyes on the Prize."

Hale Woodruff (1900–1980)

Woodruff, born in Cairo, Illinois, was the first African American to attend Indiana's Herron Art Institute. In 1926, he won second prize in the Harmon Foundation competition for painting. Woodruff studied with Mexican muralist Diego Rivera and in Paris, where his cubist style matured. He completed three mural series, *The Amistad Mutiny* for Talladega College, *The Negro in California History* for the Golden State Mutual Life Insurance Company (with Charles Alston), and *The Art of the Negro* for Clarke Atlanta University. He joined the faculty at Atlanta University, where he developed the university's art program. Later, Woodruff moved to New York to teach at New York University.

Recommended Reading

Africanus. Leo. *De totius Africae descriptione libri IX*. Translated by Jean Florian, Anvers, Jean Latium, 1556, and 1588. Re-edited in Leiden: Elzevir, 1632. African geography, history, important trade routes, and inhabitants.

Aptheker, Herbert. *American Negro Slave Revolts*. New York: Columbia University Press, 1943.
— *A Documentary History of the Negro People*, Volumes 1- 6. New York: Citadel Press, 1990.

Baldwin, James. *The Fire Next Time*. New York: Dial Press, 1963. Two masterful from-the-heart essays, of violence and hope, predicting the bloodshed in retaliation to participants of the Civil Rights Movement.

Banneker, Benjamin. *Bannaker's Pennsylvania, Delaware, Maryland, Virginia, Kentucky, and North Carolina, Almanack and Ephemeris*. Series of 6. Baltimore: Various, 1792 -1796.

Bearden, Romare, and Harry Henderson. *A History of African-American Artists: From 1792 to Present*. New York: Pantheon, 1993.

Bennett, Lerone, Jr. *Before the Mayflower: A History of the Negro in America, 1619-1962*. Chicago: Johnson Publishing, 1962.

Black Entrepreneurs of the Eighteenth and Nineteenth Centuries. Boston: Federal Reserve Bank of Boston, and Museum of African American History, Boston and Nantucket, 2009.

Blackmon, Douglas. *Slavery by Another Name: The Re-enslavement of Black Americans from the Civil War to World War II*. New York: Doubleday, 2008.

Blockson, Charles. *A Commented Bibliography on 101 Influential Books By and About People of African Descent, (1556-1982)*. Netherlands: A. Gerits & Sons, 1989.

Campbell, Mary Schmidt. Harlem Renaissance: Art of Black America. New York: Harry N. Abrams, 1994.

Capitein, Jacobus Elisa Johannes. *Staakundig-Godgeleerd Onderzoekschrift Over de Slaverny*. Amsteldam: Gerrit de Groot ,1742. This literary work contains a rare dissertation in the defense of slavery by an African orphan, educated in Holland.

Captive Passage: The Transatlantic Slave Trade and the Making of the Americas. Newport News: Smithsonian Press, Mariners Museum, 2002. This exhibition seeks to understand this maritime epic and its legacies.

Clarkson, Thomas. *The History of the Rise, Progress and Accomplishment of the Abolition of the African Slave-Trade, by the British Parliament. 2 Vols.* London: Longman, Hurst, Rees, and Orme,1808. The influences and accounting of Clarkson's long, active protest against the slave trade.

Cleaver, Eldridge. *Soul on Ice*. New York: McGraw-Hill, 1967. A deeply moving, intellectually wide-ranging, symbolic, portrayal of black life.

Diop, Cheikh Anta. *The African Origin of Civilization: Myth or Reality*. New York: L. Hill, 1974. The theory that Egypt is a civilization of Black origins.

Dodson, Howard. *Jubilee: The Emergence of African-American Culture*. Wash., D.C.: National Geographic, 2003. An illustrated study identifying the social, cultural, political, and economic factors that helped slaves from various African regions integrate their individual religions, artistic expressions, and languages into a distinctive African-American culture.

Douglass, Frederick. *Narrative of the Life of Frederick Douglass, An American Slave*. Boston: Anti-Slavery Office, 1845. A fugitive slave who became an abolitionist and a great orator of the 1800s.
—*Oration, Delivered in Corinthian Hall*. Rochester: Anti-Slavery Office, 1852. The best-known narrative of the ante-bellum period, written seven years after Douglass escaped from slavery.

Dover, Cedric. *American Negro Art*. Greenwich: NY Graphic Society, 1960.

Driskell, David. *Two Centuries of Black American Art*. New York: A. Knopf, 1976. Los Angeles County Museum of Art's 1976 exhibition, one of the first to recognize the contributions of African-American artists.
—*The Other Side of Color: African American Art in the Collection of Camille O. and William H. Cosby, Jr.* Rohnert Park: Pomegranate, 2001. Discusses prominent postcolonial African American artists and their struggles for cultural emancipation and acceptance into American mainstream.

Du Bois, W.E.B. *The Souls of Black Folk*. Chicago: A.C. McClurg, 1903. A timeless literary work highlighting the struggle that has dominated black and white Americans on the quest for dignity, justice and equality.

Dumond, Dwight. *Anti-Slavery: The Crusade for Freedom in America*. Ann Arbor: University of Michigan Press, 1961. Referencing printed anti-slavery documents - one of the most exhaustive, accurate narratives on America's victory for democracy.

Ellison, Ralph. *Invisible Man*. New York: Random House, 1952. The terrifying odyssey of one man's search for his own identity.

Equiano, Olaudah. *The Interesting Narrative of the Life of Olaudah Equiano, or Gustavus Vassa, The African*. London: T. Wilkins, 1789. A slave who earned the price of his freedom, became a world-traveling seaman, and wrote this bestseller of its time, furthering the anti-slavery cause.

Fisher, Angela. *Africa Adorned*. New York: Harry N. Abrams, 1984. A visual narrative of ceremonial African jewelry, body art and clothing, through photographs of natives from throughout the continent.

Franklin, John Hope. *From Slavery to Freedom: A History of American Negroes*. New York: A. Knopf, 1947. The often neglected history of African Americans and their impact on the formation of this nation.

Haley, Alex. *Roots*. New York: Double Day, 1976. Haley successfully traced his ancestry from a birth in 1750 in Gambia. His painstaking research, including of oral histories, opened a historical background perspective for millions of African Americans.

Hansberry, Lorraine. *A Raisin in the Sun*. New York: Random House, 1959. Exploring the courage, dignity and strength of a black family in crisis.

Holland, Jesse. *Black Men Built the Capitol: Discovering African American History In and Around Washington, D.C.* Gilford: Globe Pequot Press, 2007.

International Review of African American Art, The. Hampton, Virginia: Hampton University Museum, 1976 to present. Quarterly magazine published by the oldest African American museum (1868) in the U.S.

Johnson, Charles, Patricia Smith and WGBH Research Team. *Africans in America: America's Journey through Slavery*. New York: Harcourt Base, 1998. The indigenous history of African slavery and the involvement of Arab and European nations, and the journey of enslaved Africans across the Atlantic "Middle Passage" to the Caribbean and America.

Johnson, Walter. *Soul by Soul: Life Inside the Antebellum Slave Market*. Cambridge: Harvard University Press, 1999. The New Orleans slave market, largest in the nation, where 100,000 men, women and children were packaged, priced, and sold, and the brutal economics of trading.

Lewis, Samella. *African American Art and Artists*. Berkeley: University of California Press, 1994. An impressive representation of African American visual artists' work from the 18th century to the present. Lincoln, Abraham. *Emancipation Proclamations, Sept. 24, 1862, and Jan. 1, 1863*. Two Presidential executive orders during the Civil War.

Locke, Alain. *The Negro in Art: A Pictorial Record of the Negro Artist and of the Negro Theme in Art*. Wash., D.C.: Associates in Negro Folk Education, 1940.
—*The New Negro*. New York: A. & C. Boni, 1925. One of the most sought after works of the Harlem Renaissance.

Patton, Sharon. *African-American Art*. Oxford: Oxford University Press, 1998. Cultural diversity and synthesis of cultures making up society as a whole, as told through a myriad of African American artistic expression.

Porter, James A. *Modern Negro Art*. New York: Dryden Press, 1943. Insight to the development of African American visual artists, with multiple bibliographic references.

Powell, Richard. *Black Art: A Cultural History*. New York: Thames & Hudson, 2002.

Powell, Richard and Jock Reynolds. *To Conserve a Legacy: American Art from Historically Black Colleges and Universities*. Andover: Addison Gallery of American Art, and New York: Studio Museum of Harlem, 1999. This traveling exhibition contains works from collections of six of the oldest, most prestigious, historically black universities (Clark Atlanta, Fisk, Hampton, Howard, North Carolina Central, and Tuskegee).

Rabby, Glenda. *The Pain and the Promise: The Struggle for Civil Rights in Tallahassee, Florida*. Athens: University of Georgia Press, 1999. Florida's underappreciated involvement in the Civil Rights Movement.

Rediker, Marcus. *The Slave Ship: A Human History*. New York: Viking Penguin, 2007. Illuminates the greed, cruelty and violence inflicted upon Africans on cargo ships over four centuries.

Reynolds, Gary, Beryl Wright and David Driskell. *Against the Odds: African-American Artists and the Harmon Foundation*. Newark: Newark Museum, 1990. The 1990 Harmon Foundation Collection Exhibition.

Rhoden, William. *Forty Million Dollar Slaves: The Rise, Fall, and Redemption of the Black Athlete*. New York: Three Rivers Press, 2006.

Rivers, Larry. *Slavery in Florida -Territorial Days to Emancipation*. Gainesville: University Press of Florida, 2000. An important illustrated social history of slavery, depicting what life was like for bondservants in Florida from 1861-1865, and offering new slave and master insights.

Sancho, Ignatius. *Letters of the Late Ignatius Sancho, An African, in Two Volumes*. London: J. Nichols, 1782. Memoir of a slave who became a notable intellect, actor and author among the English elite.

Sinnette, Elinor Des Verney. *Arthur Alfonso Schomburg: Black Bibliophile & Collector*. Detroit: Wayne State University Press, 1989. The life of Schomburg, a biracial Caribbean immigrant, involved with New York radical politics, a collector of African and African American literature, and at the center of the Harlem Renaissance.

Stampp, Kenneth M. *The Peculiar Institution: Slavery in the Ante-Bellum South*. New York: Vintage/Anchor, 1956.

Stuckey, Sterling. *Slave Culture: Nationalist Theory and the Foundations of Black America*. Oxford: Oxford University Press, 1987. Remembering African influences in slave life and American culture.

Taha, Halima. *Collecting African American Art*. New York: Crown, 1998. A guide to collecting, expanding and investing in an African American art collection - including beautiful prints of artwork for fine-tuning one's knowledge of African American art.

Taney, Roger. *The Case of Dred Scott in the United States Supreme Court*. New York: Greeley & McElrath, 1857. Contains the full opinions of Chief Justice Taney and Justice Curtis, abstracts of the opinion of other judges, and analyses of points ruled.

Truth, Sojourner. *Narrative of Sojourner Truth, A Northern Slave, Emancipated from Bodily Servitude by the State of New York in 1829*. Boston: Edward O. Jenkins, 1850. The biography of an African American abolitionist and women's rights activist during the 1800s.

Washington, Booker Taliaferro. *Up From Slavery: An Autobiography*. New York: Doubleday, Page, 1901.

Wheatley, Phillis. *Poems on Various Subjects, Religious and Moral*. London: Act of Parliament, 1773. A compilation of poems by the first African American woman to publish a book.

Willis, Deborah. *Reflections in Black: A History of Black Photographers, 1840 to the Present*. New York: W.W. Norton, 2000.

Woodson, Carter. Various articles for *The Journal of Negro History*. Wash., D.C.: The Association for the Study of Negro Life and History, 1916-1940. Woodson founded this journal, still published as *The Journal of African American History*.
—*The Negro in Our History*. Wash., D.C.: Associate Publishers, Inc., 1922.

Woolman, John. *Some Considerations on the Keeping of Negroes*. Church-Alley: James Chattin, 1754. The journey of a tailor, a humanitarian who led one of the first major crusades against slavery.

Wright, Richard. *Native Son*. New York; London: Harper & Brothers, 1940. A novel about Bigger Thomas, a victim of racism and oppression.

X, Malcolm and Alex Haley. *The Autobiography of Malcolm X*. New York: Grove Press, 1975. The fascinating saga of one of the most powerful leaders of the turbulent 1950-60s.

List of Artists and Art

List of Historic Artifacts (presentation order)

List of Historic Artifacts (presentation order), *continued*

Acknowledgments

Many thanks to our corporate sponsors who believed in our mission and made this possible through their support:

Edison International—
  Southern California Edison
Toyota Motor Sales, USA, Inc.
Farmers Insurance Group
United Parcel Service of America, Inc.
Northrop Grumman Foundation
Southwest Airlines

The Bernard & Shirley Kinsey Foundation
for Arts and Education

Board members:
Adrienne N. Newsom, Attorney
Bernard W. Kinsey, Executive Director & CEO
Shirley Pooler Kinsey, President
Christopher Floyd, Treasurer
Terry D. Harris
Khalil B. Kinsey
Pamela T. Walker

Great appreciation is extended to the following friends whose voices gave life to the exhibition's cell phone tour.
Angela Bassett
Louis Gossett Jr.
Dennis Haysbert
Khalil B. Kinsey
Nichelle Nichols
Beverly Todd
Lorraine Toussaint
Courtney B. Vance
Hattie Winston

Contributors:
Special thanks for support and help from:
Charles & Doreen Allen, book producers with
  extraordinary patience and persistence
Douglas Blackmon, author and writer
Haili Francis, research assistant and writer
Susan Green, editorial consulting
Terry Harris, art consultant
Hakeem Holloway, research assistant and
  writer
Khalil Kinsey, research, editing and
  contributing writer
Jill Moniz, PhD, additional research, curatorial
  services, and preliminary copy
Emanuel Pope, videographer
Edward Pratt, art and history consultant
Richard Scott, Jr., web designer
Gary Shafner of NPA for his ongoing support of
  our mission
Gerald Tookes, videographer

Photographers:

Mikel Alatza
Charles Allen
Manuel Flores
Robert Hale
Douglas Hill
Kwesi Hutchful
Tony Leavell
Kallen Lunt
Kirk McKoy
John Sullivan
Frank Turner

Special thanks to the following directors and staff for hosting
The Kinsey Collection
in their museums:

Charmaine Jefferson, Executive Director
  California African American Museum

John Pepper, Chairman, & Don Murphy, CEO,
  National Underground Railroad Freedom
  Center

Antoinette D. Wright, President & CEO,
  DuSable Museum of African American
  History

Christina Orr-Cahall, Executive Director
  Norton Museum of Art

Chucha Barber, CEO
  Mary Brogan Museum of Art and Science,
  a Smithsonian Institution Affiliate

Brent Glass, Director
  National Museum of American History
  Smithsonian Institution

Lonnie G. Bunch III, Founding Director
  National Museum of African American
  History and Culture
  Smithsonian Institution

Family and Friends

Our gratitude and warmest appreciation is extended to the many individuals who have been generous with advice, support, and love. You are our strongest supporters and have been with us on this journey from the beginning.

Andrea Adams
Dr. James Ammons
Carmen & Kent Amos
Carl Anderson *
Sandra Dee Anderson
Jacqueline & Clarence Avant
Chucha Barber
Sherry & Tom Barrat
Congresswoman Karen Bass
Phoebe Beasley & Don Alberti
DeeDee & Bob Billingslea
Bishop Charles & Mae Blake
Beatrice & Andrea Bossi
Sylvia Wynette Bradwell
Blaun Eva & Hiram Brewton
Eula & Charles Broadnax
Darrell Brown
Doris T. & Reginald L. Brown Jr.
Anne H. & Wren T. Brown
Lonnie G. Bunch III
Laphonza Butler
Reuben Cannon
Reginald Carey
John Clayton
Marian & Ted Craver
Diane Neely Curtright
Derrick Delaney
Moneese de Lara
Sharon Drake
Ed Dwight
Dr. James Eaton *
Willis Edwards
Sandra Evers-Manley
Judy Pace Flood

Christopher Floyd
Dr. William P. Foster *
Sheila Frazier
Cassandra F. Freeman
Brenda & Bill Galloway
George Gibbs
Alonzetta Tinker Gibson
Rosalie Gordon-Mills *
Thelma & Terry Harris
Richard Hartnack
Donald Henderson
Stan Henderson
Dr. Mary Jane Hewitt
Dr. James Hill
Rosalie Hamm Hines
Dierdre & Russell Jackson
Taydra Mitchell Jackson
Benjamin Todd Jealous
Grace Jenkins
Lenita & Ronald Joe
Barbara Richardson Johnson
Julie & Joseph Johnson
Stella & Harry Jones
Alitash Kebede
John Kennedy
Allison V. Kinsey
Khalil B. Kinsey
Linda M. Kinsey
Penelope J. & Bradshaw P. Kinsey
Sheryl C. Kinsey
Cassandra Kinsey-Scott & Richard Scott
Artis Lane
Mattie & Michael Lawson
Congresswoman Barbara Lee
Dr. Samella Lewis
Bishop Wallace E. Lockett *
John E. Martin
Noel Massie
Jerry Mattes
Faye McClure
Kisten McGowan-Sims
Irv Miller

T. Damian Mitchell
Thomas L. Mitchell
Rev. Cecil L. Murray
Adrienne Newsom
Eugenia Nicholas
Danita Patterson
Ruth Plummer
Gwen Plummer-Sermon
The Albertha & Eddie Pooler Family
Julieanna Richardson
Congresswoman Laura Richardson
Dr. Larry Rivers
Evelyn Robertson
Michael Rouse
Eugene Ruffin
Katrina & Christopher Schauble
Gilbert & Brenda Scott
Bridget Sermon
Angelia & Robert Singleton
Dawnyelle Singleton
Carmen Smith
Albert Stiles
Lyn & David Talbert
David Thomas
Nancy & Larry Thompson
Phyllis & Kevin Toney
Paulette H. & Walter Tucker
Pamela & Nicholas Walker
Congresswoman Diane Watson
James A. Webster *
Eric D. White
Dr. Julian White
Kelley White-Riles
Terry & Bill Whitaker
Alfred Williams
Gloria & Michael Williams
Shawn Williams-Kinsey
Angela Robinson Witherspoon
Carolene J. & Harry Wood
Mia W. Wright

* Deceased

the Justices of the Peace for the
Augustus Keppel Falkener of the
longing to him, named Jem, an
ove said Masters Service, and
itting many Acts of Felony. —
tate, to command the said Sla
return to their said Master.
eriff of the said County of War
rsuit after the abovementioned
prehend and secure, so that they